GOODBYE TO BEDLAM

Books by John Langone

Death Is a Noun: A View of the End of Life

Goodbye to Bedlam: Understanding Mental Illness and Retardation

GOODBYE TO BEDLAM

Understanding Mental Illness
and Retardation

by John Langone

Little, Brown and Company/Boston/Toronto

Library of Congress Cataloging in Publication Data

Langone, John, 1929–
    Goodbye to bedlam.

    SUMMARY: A brief history of social attitudes
toward mental illness describing the characteristics
and treatment of specific mental disorders.
    Bibliography: p.
    1. Psychiatry--Juvenile literature.
2. Mental deficiency--Juvenile literature.
[1. Mental illness. 2. Psychiatry] I. Title.
RC454.L33   616.8'9   73-20111
ISBN 0-316-51421-7

Published simultaneously in Canada
by Little, Brown & Company (Canada) Limited

PRINTED IN THE UNITED STATES OF AMERICA

To the best kids I know, my son and daughters —
Matthew, Gia and Lisa

Contents

GOODBYE TO BEDLAM

1 Understanding Abnormality

At the turn of the century, a popular reference book that prided itself on being "authentic, comprehensive and up to date," estimated that there were 168,900 insane persons in the United States. It also listed the causes of insanity as follows:

"Heredity, 24 percent; drink, 14 percent; business, 12 percent; loss of friends, 11 percent; sickness, 10 percent; various, 12 percent."

These statistics and the rather generalized approach to cause do not, of course, mean much today what with the emphasis on walk-in psychiatric clinics, mind-altering drugs, chromosomes and DNA, sensitivity sessions and psychodrama. Today, virtually everyone who has read a psychology book or taken one course could explode the above figures. It is a time when the jargon of the psychologist, once private stock ranging from "acting out" to "withdrawal," has become the stuff of radio and television talk shows. Movies, plays, and novels have "deep psychological meaning," psychosis and neurosis are household

3

words. Everyone knows about the "shrink," and can talk about "blowing his mind," "hangups," "getting it together," and what it means to be "freaked out."

How we behave and why interest most of us tremendously. But, when a science takes hold of the popular imagination, myths and misconceptions arise (much as they do when the subject fails to interest us), and ignorance exerts its harmful influence. Mental health and mental illness are terms thrown about quite easily. They are less easily explained, and as a result many people become either instant experts after reading one magazine article, and begin to "psych" themselves or others, or do not look too closely at conditions that affect the human mind, dismissing those so afflicted as "just crazy."

Man, it appears, has long been aware that all is not always right with his psychic world. Some primitive people believed that evil spirits or the souls of their ancestors dwelt in the heads of those who were "different." And there is fossil evidence to show that some of these early people performed an operation known as trepanation, in which a hole is cut in the skull to relieve pressure on the brain in order to release the harmful spirit. The early Greeks blamed a goddess named Mania for aberrant behavior, and those who lived during the superstition-ridden Middle Ages saw derangement as the work of devils, demons, and witches, who could be cast out only by potions, torture or prayer. Always there was the notion that the mentally ill were being punished for something. In the Bible's Book of Deuteronomy, we are told that violators of the law of God will be struck with "madness and blindness and fury of mind."

With the notion that the mentally ill were possessed by

evil came mistreatment. Even as late as the reign of Henry VIII, the "Defender of the Faith," the mentally ill were tortured and beaten, notably at the infamous hospital of Saint Mary of Bethlehem in London. Founded in 1247 as a monastery, it was given to the city of London as a prison for the insane by Henry in 1547. With its name corrupted to Bedlam, a word that has entered the language to mean a scene of wild uproar and confusion, the institution was just that. "Tom o' Bedlam" was a popular expression that meant madman. In his famed diary, John Evelyn, an English author who recorded events of the 1600s, wrote: "At my returne I stept into Bedlame, where I saw several poore miserable creatures in chaines." Not only were the inmates of the notorious "hospital" chained, but they were also exhibited, like animals in a zoo, and publicly beaten and tortured for the entertainment of visitors, who paid an admission fee. One celebrated "patient" at Bedlam was James Norris, who tried to murder a guard, a crime the authorities decided to punish him for by locking him into a special device that prevented him from moving his arms. Though he could stand, sit and lie down, he could not drag himself more than a few inches from a pole to which he was chained. The unfortunate Norris stayed that way for more than a dozen years.

Gradually, attitudes toward the mentally ill began to change for the better. Even during the Middle Ages some attempts were made to care for the insane, and a number of institutions sprang up throughout Europe. Although many were an improvement over Bedlam, they were custodial for the most part, and little of importance was accomplished in the way of treatment.

It was not until the 1700s that noticeable reform was

achieved, and several pioneering humanitarians played a role in the shift. One was the French physician, Philippe Pinel, who in 1793 dramatically removed the chains from those imprisoned in the dungeonlike cells of the asylum at Bicêtre, south of Paris. Another was William Tuke, an English merchant, who founded a famed Retreat at York in 1796 for the humane treatment of a few dozen mentally ill patients. There the patients were free to move about in an atmosphere of friendliness and kindness, and were encouraged to perform manual work.

The United States, which in its early years was not much different from Europe in its citizens' attitudes toward the mentally ill, had its reformer in Dorothea Lynde Dix of Maine. In 1820, she established a school for girls in Boston, and began devoting her energies to improving the lot of paupers, prisoners, and the insane. Once, while instructing women inmates of a jail in Cambridge, Massachusetts, she noticed that the mentally ill were locked in cells in the cold and damp cellar. When she asked why there was no stove, a keeper — whose response was typical of the era's attitude — told her: "Insane people do not feel the cold."

Ms. Dix, who later served with the Union Army as a superintendent of nurses during the Civil War, visited almshouses and prisons and virtually every place in Massachusetts where the mentally ill were held, campaigning for better conditions. In a passionate speech before the State Legislature, she declared: "I proceed, gentlemen, briefly to call your attention to the present state of insane persons confined within this Commonwealth, in cages, cellars, closets, stalls, pens, chained, naked, beaten with rods and lashed into obedience." Her crusading efforts not only resulted in the building of more mental hospitals in Massachusetts, but were also responsible for the founding of institutions for the insane and the poor in twenty states and in Canada, and for an improvement in prison conditions all over Europe.

Today, while attitudes toward, and the treatment of, the mentally ill have improved markedly, the fact remains that mental illness is still very much with us.

Who are the mentally ill, and what is mental illness?

Neither question is easy to answer. But for a start, forget the terms insane, lunatic, and maniac. These are vague and now obsolete in psychiatry. While insane does generally mean a psychotic state, an unsound mind, or mental derangement, it is used mainly as a legal term. When, for instance, a murderer faces a court of law, the question is often asked, "Did he know what he was doing?" Or, "Was he insane or sane when the crime was committed?" Determining responsibility of this sort is a problem that has been debated hotly for years. In 1843, the so-called McNaghten Rule (named after a murderer who was acquitted because he was judged insane, and sometimes referred to as the "right and wrong test") came into being in an attempt to resolve the conflict over responsibility. Under McNaghten, which was widely used, a jury was required only to consider whether a defendant knew the difference between right and wrong. If he did not, he was ruled legally insane. One pitfall in this was that the rule did not consider that a defendant might be held to be insane even though he did know the difference and was acting under an irresistible impulse, which can, and does, occur.

In 1954 the Durham Rule was drafted. More in line

7

with modern psychiatric thought than the earlier tests of legal responsibility, it broadened the concept of insanity as a defense by stating that the criminal was not responsible if his unlawful act was the product of mental disease or defect. Under Durham, a psychiatrist is permitted to testify about the mental illness at issue, instead of simply confining his views to whether the defendant knew right from wrong. The test proceeds on the assumption that when a criminal act stems from the defendant's mental illness, the suggested conclusion is that he should be hospitalized, treated, and, hopefully, rehabilitated.

If mental illness is not merely another word for insanity, not being "just crazy" or possessed by devils, what is it exactly and who gets it? Dr. Jonathan Cole, superintendent of Boston State Hospital, was once asked these questions, and his response was a testimonial to their complexity. "Mental illness is something that even psychiatrists have trouble defining today," he said. "The definition is in an acute state of confusion. Mental illness has boundary problems. It may be an obnoxious label. Many of our clients are people in distress."

There are officially approved lists of diseases and disorders on which are included many of the conditions of the mind we know as mental illness. But there also are health professionals who feel the standard listings are too narrow; they would broaden them to include a greater range of personality disturbances and problems. Hence, because of this difference of opinion over what truly constitutes mental illness, it is difficult to determine just how many people are so affected.

One widely held estimate is that one out of ten, or approximately 20 million Americans, suffer from mental

8

illness of varying degrees of severity. Hundreds of thousands are in mental hospitals (it has been generally accepted that one out of every two hospital beds in the country is now occupied by a mentally ill person, but the census is declining due to a new emphasis on short-term treatment on a "revolving door" basis in the community). Many more are seen by private psychiatrists and psychologists. There are, however, more than a thousand patients for every psychiatrist, which means that only a relatively small percentage of those who need help get it. More than a million children in the United States, according to the National Association for Mental Health, suffer from severe emotional disturbances; many of them, as young as two and three, suffer from mental illness as severe as that experienced by the most seriously ill adult in mental hospitals.

Further, mental illness and other personality disturbances play major roles in murder and other criminal behavior, in delinquency, suicide, alcoholism, and in drug addiction, and are important factors in 75 percent of all accidents. During World War II, about 40 percent of the young men of draft age were rejected because of nervous or mental disorders; in one study conducted in midtown Manhattan, some 75 percent of those examined displayed significant symptoms of anxiety, and one out of seven either was undergoing treatment for emotional disorders or sorely in need of treatment. The cost of all of this runs into the billions. At least $4 billion is spent annually in the United States for the treatment and prevention of mental illness, and there is a loss of around $17 billion to the economy due to the lesser productivity of the mentally ill.

Goodbye to Bedlam

The statistics are ample evidence that mental illness is a leading illness, regarded by many professionals as the chief health problem in the United States. Dr. David Rosenthal, a psychologist at the National Institute of Mental Health, said recently that evidence is growing that almost no family in the nation is entirely free of mental disorders. He suggested further that such disorders may be important factors when considering the causes of the nation's social unrest, crime, and racial disorder. "The magnitude and gravity of the mental illness problem," he said, "has relevance to the psychological turbulence rampant in an American society that is confused, divided, concerned about its future, and casting about for workable solutions to critical problems."

Dr. W. Walter Menninger of the famed Menninger Clinic in Topeka, Kansas, put it another way, "The oft-quoted ratio of one out of ten persons needing psychiatric services should be one out of one." All of us, said Dr. Menninger, have periods of emotional maladjustment or emotional illness. We lose our tempers, "blow our cool," and suffer periods of depression. While not too serious, these spells cause "off" days, days we cannot work, and sometimes these emotional blowups upset others. For some, these tense periods do not last, and life soon returns to normal. For others, those with serious mental problems, life becomes a burden; they sink deeper into depression, lose their ability to snap back and to carry on, behave in strange ways, and often split with reality.

Broadly speaking, while there are many conditions of the mind that qualify as mental illness, there are two major types, organic and functional. Organic disorders are those caused by physical disturbance of brain function, such as injury before birth, infection, chemical action, or a tumor. The functional ones are those with an emotional origin and with no apparent changes in the brain. As we shall see throughout this book, while most mental illnesses are considered to be functional, there is a growing body of evidence linking organic causes to abnormal and subnormal behavior.

There are three major categories of mental illness: psychoses, neuroses, and a somewhat shadowy group known as character disorders. We will focus on the psychoses in the remainder of this chapter.

Psychoses are serious mental disorders, what most people think of when someone uses the word insane. They are of organic and/or emotional origin and prevent the sufferer from behaving in a socially acceptable way. A person with a major psychosis does not follow the usual patterns of thinking, feeling, and acting. He is out of touch with reality; he sees things in a different and distorted way; he loses control of his impulses; and he suffers from delusions and hallucinations.

Chief among the psychoses is schizophrenia, the largest single category of the mentally ill, a mind-crippler that splits the person so afflicted from the real world, jumbles his thoughts, and twists his emotions.

Another major psychosis is manic-depression. This psychosis is actually a group of problems characterized by marked swings in mood from elation and excitability to melancholy so deep that the person may entertain suicidal thoughts or may even be struck dumb and rendered immobile. Some people may only be manic, or "high," without ever being depressed, while others may be constantly depressed without experiencing a manic phase. Manic-depressive psychosis may also take a milder form, and many patients have made good recoveries from it. Recently, scientists at Columbia-Presbyterian Medical Center in New York found evidence that some manic-depression can be inherited via the X chromosome, one of the sex chromosomes, those carriers of genetic material and information.

Paranoia is another type of psychosis. It also is a type of schizophrenia, as we shall see, and in its "pure" form it is rather rare. Paranoia comes on slowly, enveloping the sufferer in unchanging and well-organized delusions of persecution or grandeur that become the most believable part of his daily life. The paranoid individual is suspicious, and believes people are plotting against him. Obviously, everyone at one time or another develops suspicions — some founded, others not — but this perfectly normal trait should not be confused with the deteriorated mental state of the true paranoid whose suspicions have so festered that he often physically assails those he believes are tormenting him. The cause of the disease is not totally clear, but it has been suggested that the paranoiac is narcissistic; that is, he has developed an intense love of himself. Unable to find fault with himself, his confused mind seeks a scapegoat, setting up suspicions and delusions of persecution. Some psychiatrists say that what the paranoiac is doing is defending his first love, himself.

Still another psychosis is senile dementia, a mental state that afflicts the very old. This gradual deterioration of the personality and memory leaves the person irritable, eccentric, and without control of his emotions. This condition is caused by the wasting away of the brain due to the relentless aging process. Dementia, a term once used to describe insanity that now refers to organic disorders of the mind, may also result from hardening of the arteries in the brain, or cerebral arteriosclerosis.

General paresis is another psychosis associated with organic brain disease. Caused by syphilitic infection of the nervous system, the disease brings on gradual paralysis, an inability to concentrate, personality changes, and often a manic state with grandiose delusions.

Another example of how a psychosis may be linked to physical upset of the brain was reported at a 1972 meeting of the Radiological Society of North America. Discussing a follow-up study involving 4,198 patients tested at the New York University Medical Center for ringworm of the scalp, Dr. Melvin Becker noted that there was a small but significantly higher incidence of mental illness in patients who had had radiation treatment. Of the 4,198 patients, 2,404 were given X-ray scalp therapy and 1,794 received treatment without radiation. Follow-up time after treatment averaged fifteen years and the mean age of the patients at the time of treatment, between 1940 and 1958, was seven years. Mental illness, mostly psychosis, was reported in 9.5 percent of the patients treated with radiation and in 5.3 percent of the control group, those treated without. The doctor said that prior to the study, there was no reported association of mental illness in patients who had had radiation exposure of the head. He added that there was no apparent answer for the noticeably higher incidence of mental illness, but that in addition to the possibility of radiation damage to the brain, the baldness that followed radiation treatment might have caused the psychic trauma.

Goodbye to Bedlam

It should be noted that the lines that separate the categories of mental illness are not stone walls. The terms psychosis, neurosis, and character disorder are simply labels, and while they are obviously necessary, there are so many degrees of severity in each category (along with borderline states that defy definition) that it would be foolhardy to try to assign every bit of off-beat behavior its own neatly mapped territory. The human mind and feelings are far too intricate for such simple treatment, and we know too little about how and why human beings act the way they do to be doctrinaire. As the Swiss psychologist and psychiatrist Carl Gustav Jung put it, "Even if everyone knows how everything in a given person has come about, that person would still be only half understood."

Everybody is prone to mental illness, the great as well as the unheralded. The famed artists Vincent Van Gogh, Paul Gauguin, and Amedeo Modigliani all had a mental illness of one kind or another; none of their problems, however, marred their creativity. President Lincoln suffered a schizophrenic breakdown in his youth and was plagued by melancholy, and President Rutherford B. Hayes often dissolved into fits of weeping. Each of us, then, has within ourself and in our environment the ingredients that can push us over the brink into psychosis. We each have a built-in tolerance to stress, but we also have a breaking point, and for some of us the point at which we shatter is arrived at quickly.

What must be understood is that mental illness is a matter of *degree*, that the problems of those we call mentally ill differ only in *degree* from the problems of those we know as normal — a word that has come to

14

mean "free from any mental disorder, sane," but whose meaning is actually rather nebulous.

Above all, it is important to realize that mental illness is not a state someone brings deliberately upon himself. The patient generally has no control over what has happened to his mind until he undergoes treatment, no more than he has control over many of the diseases that strike him. Nor is the person who seeks help for a mental problem a weakling. In the pages ahead we will examine some of the other kinds, causes, and treatments of mental illness and, hopefully, try to dispel a few myths and misconceptions about one of the most common forms of disease.

2 Neuroses

Everyone has his "down" days. In fact, if we did not, if we went merrily through life with never a twinge of anxiety or depression, if we never experienced fits of jealousy, hatred, fear, guilt, and inferiority, we would be considered abnormal.

But there are times when these normal reactions get out of hand, and begin to engulf a person. He finds it hard to enjoy life and relate to his friends, thrown off course as he is by the nagging tenseness and edginess that continually interrupt his sleep, ruin his appetite, and cause a variety of physical ills. This unhappy person is neurotic. He suffers from a neurosis, or psychoneurosis, as the disorder often is called.

Neuroses are the most common of the many forms of mental illness, and are generally regarded as mild disorders. That is, they are usually less severe than the psychoses. The neurotic individual is not as out of touch with reality as is the psychotic, and he is usually painfully aware of the conflict that is churning his mind. There are many types of neuroses and, again, many borderline states. But central to each is anxiety, that uneasiness of mind caused by anticipation of danger or misfortune. Anxiety can have its origin in some outside event, as when a mother fears for the safety of her son serving on a war-torn battlefield. Or it can arise within the individual's mind with no apparent cause or out of proportion to any external forces, and this can be more serious.

Conflict is at the root of anxiety. A child, for example, may be overprotected, pampered, and stifled by doting parents. Later in life, he finds himself exposed to the ordinary problems and situations that everyone must face, but from which he has been shielded. His rather comfortable and ordered existence is jarred. A conflict begins to brew in his unconscious, the part of the mind that contains material of which we are not aware. One inner voice urges him to seek shelter in the security of the past and shut out the particular problem facing him. This voice is that of the id, in Freudian theory the portion of the personality that controls our desires and our primitive instincts, such as self-preservation. Another voice advises him to grow up, that society does not approve of such childish behavior. This voice belongs to the superego, or conscience, that part of the personality allied with standards and self-criticism. He tries to resolve the emotional conflict raging within him but finds himself mentally frozen. He becomes high-strung, restless, apprehensive. It is a painfully disagreeable feeling, and its weight is often unbearable.

There are times, of course, when anxiety can help us get things done, and we need a certain amount of it to enable us to respond to some situations. Anxious people may also be creative, fired with ambition and drive, and it has been said that the world is full of apparently happy and valuable individuals who can thank concealed neurotic forces for their achievements. But these same forces can cause mental and physical ills and, as a result, our behavior is altered. (The term psychosomatic is used to describe physical ailments brought on by emotional disturbance; these will be discussed in Chapter 6.) A child suffering from severe anxiety may bite his nails or wet his bed. On a battlefield, the combat soldier's mind is also churned by various stresses. He may find himself torn between the counsel of his two inner instincts, the one of self-preservation that urges him to throw down his rifle and run, and the social instinct, buoyed by a waving flag or a blaring brass band, which tells him that he, too, can be a hero, that to be appreciated and admired is important, that there are things one must do for the good of one's comrades. Those soldiers who were unable to break out of the dilemma were struck down by what we call war neuroses.

Because anxiety is such an intolerable sensation, the sufferer tries to rid himself of it. And in the psychic fight to do this he employs what are known as defense mechanisms. These are tools we use everyday in some form to cope with our problems; they work in much the same way as our bodies do when they react against some invading virus or bacteria to protect against infection. Some defense mechanisms are conscious acts, but true ones are unconscious; that is, the person who uses them to allay anxiety and emotional strife does not know he is doing so.

Defense mechanisms are the responsibility of the ego, the third part of Freudian psychic apparatus. This is the self, the "I," the part of the personality that keeps an individual aware of reality. The ego modifies behavior by making compromises, by mediating, between the primitive drives of the id and the bans and demands of the superego and the physical environment. The ego does not particularly like being attacked. When something occurs that threatens the ego, it becomes uncomfortable and guilty and, under stress, calls various defense mechanisms into play.

One of the most common of these is repression, which banishes unacceptable ideas, memories, and impulses from our consciousness. A person who uses repression as a defense against painful sources of anxiety unwittingly relegates them to his unconscious and is not able to remember them easily. But the mind has been likened to a piece of unexposed film, and any event that occurs is captured on that film. So, while repression may be a successful defense, some of the repressed thoughts may burst out later, perhaps in another shape. A pyromaniac, for example, who has a morbid compulsion to set fires, may be a sexually repressed person who experiences compensating sexual excitement from setting or watching a blaze.

Denial is another defense mechanism. Those who use this approach might refuse to acknowledge that some real and unbearable problem exists. There is also rationalization, an attempt to explain and justify behavior while at the same time hiding the real motives. Projection is yet another defense, in which a person rejects what is emotionally distasteful in himself and attributes it to others because his ego cannot tolerate the discomfort. A paranoid person would employ such a defense, but so, too, would a normal person. In displacement, still another defense, the individual transfers an emotion from one object to an acceptable substitute. A baseball player, for instance, angered at going hitless, may displace his anger onto his bat and slam it to the ground. Reaction formation is a defense mechanism by which a person assumes an attitude or behavior that is just the opposite of impulses he is fighting. He may, for example, have strong inward leanings to be a nonconformist and to be inconsiderate, and he reacts by forming a deeply moral and religious exterior. In sublimation, another defense, unacceptable instincts are rerouted toward more socially acceptable goals. It has been pointed out that individuals often sublimate a strong sexual impulse — an example of a stern superego clashing with a restless id to bring about a compromise — by turning to creative work in art and music.

Some people may turn against themselves as a defense. They unconsciously reflect back onto themselves an attitude or an emotion that had been directed at someone else. For instance, a person who may have lost faith in a close friend because of some displeasing act might lose faith in himself.

While some of these defenses are helpful and enable us to keep our emotions on a relatively even keel, there are times when they run out of control, resulting in neurosis. There are many neuroses, each tailor-made, as it were, to the inherited and acquired characteristics of an individual.

One of the most common is called an obsessive-compulsive reaction. Those plagued by it have uncontrollable urges to repeat certain acts or to think the same ideas over and over again as they attempt to break the grip of anxiety by substituting one form of behavior for another hidden, unacceptable kind. Or, they perform the acts to pay for a "sin" or to reassure themselves that all is well. An obsessive-compulsive person might wash his hands dozens of times in a day. He might bolt a door, walk away from it, and return to check that it has been locked securely — and he will repeat this ritual several times. He might read and reread a paragraph in a book so many times that it loses its meaning, or he might be compelled to count every single tree on a street each time he goes for a walk. When such behavior is carried to an extreme it can be as restricting as a severe physical illness, for if the sufferer fails to repeat the particular act his anxiety is heightened.

Hysteria is another neurosis, and is a term attributed to the Greek "Father of Medicine," Hippocrates, who believed that emotional disturbances were peculiar to women. The word hysteria is derived from the Greek *hystera,* which means womb. Hippocrates' notion was considered credible for years, and a hysterectomy, an operation to remove the uterus, or womb, was considered the treatment for hysteria up to fifty years ago.

Hysteria is a common neurosis that occurs when an individual uses the defense mechanism of conversion to transform his anxiety into physical symptoms. He may, for example, suffer paralysis in his arm out of guilt for repressed violent tendencies. Symptoms of hysteria are varied. Convulsions, paralysis, numbness, fits of crying and laughter — these are all characteristic of the condition. A Duke University psychiatrist tells the story of a woman whose car struck and injured a child who had run into the roadway. Within two days, the woman lost peripheral vision in her right eye — the side from which the child approached the car.

Hypochondria is another neurosis, one that probably needs little explanation. The hypochondriac translates his anxieties into constant complaints about aches, pains, and symptoms of diseases, most of them imagined. Any unusual mental or bodily twinge sends him dashing to his physician, who usually finds no organic basis for the complaint. Undeterred, the hypochondriac often will visit doctor after doctor, seeking a cure for a disorder that does not exist. Many hypochondriacs do not actually want to be freed of their symptoms since they can be a way of arousing sympathy.

Hypochondria is related to a neurosis called neurasthenia. A person with neurasthenia feels tired and inadequate. He may remain in bed for the better part of a day, complaining that he is too weak to function. No matter how much he rests, his fatigue remains. Like the hypochondriac, there is no physical basis for his state. Once thought to be brought on by actual weakness of the nervous system, psychiatrists now know that neurasthenia has an emotional origin, that the exhaustion has developed in place of the anxiety the sufferer is trying to shed.

Phobias are another form of neurosis. Phobics shift their anxiety to some external object that becomes a symbol of their emotional conflict. The defense mechanism known as displacement is employed here. There are more than 200 phobias, each marked by a nagging, unrealistic fear of something. By being afraid of such things as heights (acrophobia) and strangers (xenophobia), the phobic avoids them, and thus the anxiety they represent. Some other common phobias are: agoraphobia, of open spaces; ailurophobia, fear of cats; algophobia, of pain; arachnephobia, of spiders; astrapophobia, of lightning;

bacteriophobia, of germs; bathophobia, of falling from high places; claustrophobia, of closed-in places; climaco-phobia, of falling downstairs; cynophobia, of dogs; demo-phobia, of crowds; dromophobia, of crossing the street; gamophobia, of marriage; hemophobia, of the sight of blood; lyssophobia, of going insane; mysophobia, of dirt; necrophobia, of the dead; ophidiophobia, of snakes; pan-phobia, of everything; photophobia, of light; rhabdo-phobia, of being beaten; scotophobia, of darkness; topo-phobia, of situations; toxicophobia, of being poisoned; triskaidekaphobia, of the number 13; zoophobia, of ani-mals.

Neurotic depression, a common neurosis, is not as seri-ous as psychotic depression, although it can lead to this. Grief caused by the loss of a loved one can bring on depression, which is normal. Carried further in a neurosis, however, depression may mean a loss of appetite and sleep, an inability to make decisions, feeling "down" for no apparent reason, and a lack of interest in life. It is a factor in many of the 22,000 suicides and 200,000 suicide attempts in the United States every year; it also figures in the widespread use of drugs, as well as being a cause of dropping out of high school and college. In fact, it has been estimated that over fifteen million people in this country suffer from mental disorders in which depression plays a star role.

Depression is not limited to adults, either. "Children are very susceptible to depression in the first year of their lives," Dr. Marie Meierhofer, a Swiss child psychiatrist, reported recently in *Medical Tribune*. "This is so because they are extremely sensitive to change. It is hard for them to adapt to new people and new surroundings." Dr.

Meierhofer added that depression was common in infants no more than three months old, especially in children who have been placed in nurseries by working mothers. How could Dr. Meierhofer tell that an infant was depressed? To make the diagnosis, she filmed 500 babies in nurseries and recognized a number of symptoms. These included a low level of activity, apparent apathy, and a characteristic expression composed of pursed lips and a wrinkled forehead. The children often cried and covered their eyes when approached. "A small child can express itself only physically," the doctor said, "and with training, depression can be recognized by observing facial expressions and behavior."

Depression also has been produced in animal studies, and researchers know that infant monkeys, like human children, go through distinct stages when separated from mothers and peers. Dr. William T. McKinney, a psychiatrist at the University of Wisconsin Medical Center, reported to the American Association for the Advancement of Science's 1970 convention that various degrees of depression had been brought on in monkeys by separating them from their mothers at various ages and under a variety of circumstances. The severity of their depressive reaction, he said, depends on a number of variables, such as age at the time of separation, the social environment from which the animal was removed, and the situation during the separation period. It was found that the first few days were characterized by intense protest at separation. The infant then "gave up" and entered a despair stage, which included huddling and self-clasping behavior. When reunited, there was increased clinging to another animal. The researchers cautioned that depression may not be the only reaction to separation, and may occur only under specific conditions. Their work did confirm clinical observations which indicated that age and prior experience were important variables in determining responses to separation.

In another study of more than two hundred depressives in New Haven, Connecticut, researchers found that their median age was in the thirties, and that 40 percent were under thirty. According to Dr. Gerald Klerman, professor of psychiatry at Harvard Medical School, a similar trend showing a decrease in the age of depressed patients has been observed at mental health facilities and state hospitals in several states. He also noted that the symptoms of depression in younger patients were strikingly similar to what has come to be called social alienation. "Alienation involves feelings of discouragement, separation from the larger social group, criticism of the existing social values, and feelings of rootlessness," he told a scientific symposium. "How similar these are to the characteristic cognitive changes associated with the mood changes of depression — hopelessness, helplessness, withdrawal from social participation, loss of interest in activities, and drop in self-esteem." He suggested that the children of such groups as blacks, Puerto Ricans, and American Indians have begun to question society's foundations, and that their feelings of alienation and despair might be related to the gap between achievement and desire. Unsuccessful in changing the social order, these young people often become depressed, disappointed, and discouraged, and some seek psychiatric help.

More recently, Michigan State University social scientists reported that they believed boys and girls of sixteen need a lot more love because they are more apt to be depressed at that age than during their other teen years because of crucial educational and career decisions. Professors Arthur M. Vener and Cyrus R. Stewart studied more than 4,000 adolescents and found that sixteen-year-olds, and to a lesser degree youths thirteen to seventeen, were not generally bored or discouraged. However, half said they sometimes did not care what happened to them, that their lives felt empty and not worth much. Sixteen-year-old girls seemed to be most affected by these feelings. The social scientists told a meeting of the American Sociological Association that they also found that adolescent stress varied with the environment. In communities of professional families and of blue-color workers, sixteen was the age of greatest stress. But in semirural working class communities, the youths were relatively stable at fourteen, fifteen, and sixteen, but seemed to be depressed in their final year of junior high school, when they were thirteen or younger, or at seventeen in their senior year of high school.

In a somewhat similar vein, Dr. R. A. Sandison of Knowle Hospital, Fareham, Hampshire, in Great Britain observed in an address in Southampton in 1972: "The decline of religious observance, the loosening of social controls, increased leisure and increasing breakdown of family life are often said to be associated with despair and loss of hope. It is more likely that changes in society and the growth and movement of populations have contributed by breaking up old settled neighborhoods, by separating the young from the extended family, and by creating urban conditions favouring loneliness and social isolation."

Some, like Dr. Harold M. Visotsky, a Northwestern University psychiatrist, believe that emotional depression is developing into an epidemic that carries with it the seeds of political demagoguery. Dr. Visotsky reasons that as depression spreads there will be more autocratic leadership as people become more apathetic about politics and refuse to choose between the things that affect their lives. Noting that the German people were both financially and emotionally depressed just before Hitler assumed power, Dr. Visotsky warns that once depression becomes a response to stress, it will continue to be a response throughout an individual's life. He blames wars and the rapidity of technological, social, and political change for leaving the young feeling powerless to control their lives. "They feel empty and vacuous and develop a sense of futility. If what a man wants and what a man feels can make no difference, then he gives up wanting and feeling. Apathy sets in. It is usually a defense against anxiety. Occasionally, it spills over and leads to destruction."

Depression, like many mental ailments, may be treated with drugs. In fact, depressive disorders have been linked to a deficiency of the hormone norepinephrine. But often these medications only mask the problem, which can surface again, just as pain does when the dulling edge of morphine wears off. The depressed person may need psychotherapy to help him get to the root of his problems and put him back into the mainstream. He also needs close friendship and understanding, a kindred spirit, someone who can lift him, let him know in countless ways that life, despite its ups and downs, is worth living; that spring does, indeed, come back; that it is wiser to anticipate and savor moments than to expect and demand sheer bliss every day of our lives.

3 Character Disorders

G. K., male, 36, chronic alcoholic who becomes psychotic under the influence of alcohol. Has no motivation for R$_x$ (therapy) and states openly that he will continue to be a drunkard.

R. S., male, 24, previously admitted for study but went AWOL. A master manipulator, he has a knack for sabotaging treatment and has been involved with and misused every facility at the hospital.

T. T., female, 21, a well-known drug addict who has been a patient intermittently for several years. Often defects and, when a patient, refuses to cooperate in any treatment program.

W. F., male, 30, a severe character disorder, dangerous and threatening. Drinks, makes suicidal gestures, threatens staff members.

The preceding capsule descriptions are from actual admitting office records at a state hospital. They describe some of the people who fall into the third major category of mental illness, character (or personality) disorders. The most severely afflicted of these individuals are called psychopaths, or sociopaths. They may well be the largest group of mentally ill because most of them are never hospitalized. Many end up in jail, charged with all sorts of antisocial behavior from writing bad checks to sexual deviation. The person who suffers from a severe character disorder (again, there are degrees, and not everyone who gets into trouble is a psychopath) is totally irresponsible, totally selfish. He never feels remorse for what he has done to himself or to others as he lies, cheats, and rebels against authority and discipline. "Nice guys finish last" is his motto, and the emotions of love, loyalty, and sympathy are alien to his mind. Tragically, he refuses to learn from experience, and because of this and because many professionals question whether he is truly mentally ill, he often is shut out of treatment programs. Shunted from hospital to hospital, jail to jail, the psychopath travels in a gray world, a bit too sick for prison, not sick enough for the mental hospital. He could be a man like Adolf Hitler, or a gunman who kills on contract. Or he shows his maladjustment by turning to drugs or alcohol, to sexual perversions or habitual criminal acts. The sociopath is most difficult to treat, and many institutions, unfortunately, do not even bother to try.

In a series of newspaper articles a few years ago, this writer called attention to a highly questionable practice that had somehow developed in Massachusetts mental hospitals, one that highlighted the difficulty in defining just who the mentally ill are and how best to handle them. It also demonstrated the differences of opinion among psychiatrists. As outmoded as the shackles that once bound mental patients to the walls of their cells, the practice involved an unpublicized administrative edict known unofficially as "the blacklist." Its purpose was to keep certain patients out of the hospital, ostensibly because they were not considered mentally ill. Aside from the psychiatrists who enforced it and the patients who were affected by it, few outside the hospital were aware of its existence. Touched by the blacklist were those classified variously as "character disorders," "window-breakers," "borderline cases," or alcoholics. Their names, along with the reasons why they should not be admitted, were often written on dog-eared sheets of paper in a loose-leaf notebook, or taped to the pullout tray in admitting office desks. More important, however, was the fact that the list, once established, had surprising longevity — more often than not in the minds of residents and psychiatric trainees whose memories about particularly troublesome patients were long — even after a hospital might decide to abolish the list. What it all meant was that a blacklisted patient stood little chance of being readmitted to a hospital, even though he might have developed a serious psychosis or suicidal depression between the time he was last discharged and that of his reapplication for admission. The blacklist said simply that the patient should not be admitted. (One such patient was described this way: "F. E. This male, 36, was recently discharged after evaluation and a diagnosis of personality disorder, addiction, also alcoholism. Decided that hospital would not offer anything for this patient, and that he should not be at this hospital. He could be assaultive. It is felt that due to the nature of his disorder and the fact that hospital cannot afford him any treatment this patient should not be readmitted.") Critics of the list, which was subsequently abolished, according to state officials, maintained that it amounted to a total denial of the idea that a patient can get well, or that he can become more ill than before. The list, in effect, tagged a patient as hopeless or, in the private jargon of interns and residents who are somewhat less than delighted at working with this type of person with whom the hospital does not get along, a "crock," or "crud."

One critic of the blacklist, Dr. Vernon Patch, a psychiatrist on the Harvard Medical School faculty, has charged that the blacklist was created for "reasons that are as obvious as the professional ethics are obscure. It is created to protect the mental hospital and its personnel from the frustrating, troublesome or unmanageable behavior of patients who are difficult to treat." Blacklist patients, he went on, can fall into any of the customary psychiatric categories; they are not simply psychopaths who should be dealt with in prison. A chronic schizophrenic who repeatedly cuts him- or herself superficially with glass or razor blades is as apt to be blacklisted for "troublesome" behavior as is the window-breaking psychopath. Also, said the doctor, alcoholism and drug addiction, both major mental health problems, have many representatives on the lists. "If a patient has made a nuisance of himself at one hospital in the state system, then another hospital should be made easily available for his care. It is no secret to mental hospital administrators that every hospital has a particular style and a particular staff, either of which may separately or together interact with the patient in such a way as to provoke the troublesome behavior or contribute to therapeutic failure. If a patient has demonstrated that his behavior is too assaultive or destructive for a particular hospital, then transfer to another institution should be considered for a therapeutic trial rather than a blacklist solution."

Hospital officials have maintained that while it is true that those responsible for clinical admissions use their judgment in admitting patients, there is no residual blacklist, nor is it a refusal of care. "It is an evaluation of how our resources can best be used," explained Dr. John Snell, director of admissions at Boston State Hospital. "The decision for admission was generally made out in the community, through the family, the doctor and so on. This is inappropriate if you're really concerned with the patient's best interests. This essentially says that the hospital doesn't have the personnel to screen. The person is admitted by default and evaluated later. Now we provide a team to do examinations, at the point when the patient arrives. We are trying to get away from the old plan which orders either 'admit' or 'refuse.' Now we don't refuse anyone. The decision as to the kind of care should ideally be made here. Whether it should be admission or care of another kind, such as at home, should be made here." Dr. Snell added that for a hospital to subscribe to the practice of admitting a person who by all the laws of society should be in prison is a tragic mistake. "What you're saying is that since prison is no good, we'll restructure his problem, and call it mental illness. The answer to this, obviously, is prison reform, and development of a new hospital or institution." He said that the type of person who appears on the blacklist is not just a problem for psychiatrists, but for the courts, the police, the church. "If the mental institutions continue to assume the burden of dealing with them," he added, "we are postponing a solution. A dialogue is needed."

And to that, Dr. Patch responded, "At the present time, care of the mentally ill is the responsibility of the state and is delegated to the Department of Mental Health. With privilege of leadership goes responsibility. Thus, it seems clear that if a dialogue is needed between the community and the mental health center or state hospital regarding better ways to deal with patients who are troublesome, frustrating, assaultive or who just don't get along well, the burden rests with the mental health professionals."

To return to the personality disorders themselves, there are many kinds; one of these is homosexuality. The homosexual is sexually attracted to members of his or her own sex, but such an individual is not and must not be regarded as immoral or degenerate. Unfortunately, too often homosexuals are the butt of off-color jokes by those who have not risen above a street-corner mentality, and the object of much legal and moral harassment. The names by which they are known are legion – gay, fruit, faggot, fairy, queen, queer, dyke (a female homosexual). In the view of many who have studied it, homosexuality should be seen as a medical problem that is treatable, not as a matter for the police or the moralists. They also feel it is wrong to classify homosexuality as a sociopathic disorder, pointing out that not every homosexual lacks conscience, a trait characteristic of the psychopath. Many homosexuals, on the other hand, reject the idea that they are "sick" and attempt to make homosexuality as accepted a form of social behavior as heterosexuality (sexual feeling toward persons of the opposite sex). Such homosexuals insist that they cannot and do not want to change, that they are homosexual because of some glandular imbalance, and they ask that the courts and the community recognize this.

Still a hush-hush topic in many homes — much as sex in general and death are — homosexuality is nevertheless very much with us. And in the eyes of specialists like Dr. Charles W. Socarides of the Albert Einstein College of Medicine, it has reached epidemic proportions. Writing in the May 18, 1970, issue of the *Journal of the American Medical Association,* Dr. Socarides, who has treated homosexuals for more than fifteen years, said that a conservative estimate was that between 2.5 and 4 million males suffer from the condition. Its frequency, he added, surpassed that of the nation's four major illnesses from 1963 to 1965: heart disease (3,619,000); arthritis and rheumatism (3,481,000); impairment (except paralysis) of the back (1,769,000); and mental and nervous disease (1,767,000). Other estimates put the number of male homosexuals in the country as high as 8 million, with female homosexuals about a third of that.

It is Dr. Socarides' contention that true homosexuality is a form of psychiatric or emotional illness, and that its only effective treatment is psychotherapy. In his report, he noted also that homosexuality is learned, acquired behavior; it is not innate or instinctual. And he disagrees that homosexuality should be granted acceptance as a valid form of sexual functioning, different from but equal to heterosexuality. Equally misleading, he adds, is the

34

idea that homosexuality is merely an aspect of normal development, a transient stage of adolescence. Dr. Socarides defines a homosexual as a person who consistently and from inner necessity engages in homosexual acts. "This pattern arises from faulty sexual identity, a product of the earliest years of life," he explains. "Typically, we find a pathological family constellation in which there is a domineering, crushing mother who will not allow the developing child to achieve autonomy from her, and an absent, weak or rejecting father."

Another view of what causes homosexuality was recently advanced by researchers working at the New England Deaconess Hospital and at Washington University School of Medicine in St. Louis. Their work, reported in the *New England Journal of Medicine* (November 18, 1971), challenges the idea that the disorder is brought on by environmental factors, particularly the father-mother role. The investigators compared 30 male homosexuals with a control group of 50 heterosexuals. They found that the homosexuals had sharply lower levels of the male hormone, testosterone, in their blood. (Testosterone, produced by the male sex glands, is responsible for such male characteristics as a deep voice and hair growth and also for the function of certain reproductive organs.) The 30 homosexuals studied by Dr. Robert C. Kolodny and his colleagues were volunteers, college students between the ages of eighteen and twenty-four. All were unmarried and in good academic standing. Two-thirds recalled happy childhoods and more than two-thirds saw their father as the dominant parent. The researchers cautioned, however, against any generalizations about the entire homosexual population, saying that they did not regard homosexuality as a disease but as a variant of sexual behavior, and that they were not suggesting that endocrine abnormalities would be found in the great majority of homosexuals.

In another study, Dr. Ray B. Evans, an associate professor of psychiatry at Loma Linda University School of Medicine in California, confirmed that childhood parental relationships of many homosexual men appear less desirable than those of heterosexual men, but said that such an observation does not establish a causal connection. Rather, he believes, the man who becomes homosexual is probably born with a genetic, biological, or biochemical difference from other men. He speculated that perhaps certain environmental factors are also necessary in addition to the biological predisposition. But he feels the particular experiences crucial to the development of homosexuality have not been verified. In his report, in *Medical Aspects of Human Sexuality* (May, 1971), Dr. Evans concluded that parental influence alone has not been proved sufficient to cause this development in their sons; however, he did not deny the contribution of parents to the problems of their children.

Despite the differences of opinion over the cause, the fact remains that physicians do try to help homosexuals, and most attempt to swerve them back toward heterosexuality and away from acceptance of their problem. It has been estimated that by using drugs and group therapy, between a third and a half of the homosexuals under treatment may be successfully converted to what society considers normal. In a report in *Medical World News,* Dr. John Money, a Johns Hopkins Hospital psychiatrist, advised other physicians faced with the medical problem that normal sexual orientation can be guided, especially around age three, by the gentle discouragement by parents of effeminate activities and the reinforcement of masculine ones. "To wait until adolescence to pay it serious attention is to give gender misorientation more time to affect the behavior of the individual permanently," he said. "The earlier the symptoms are recognized and treated, the greater the hope of a lasting change." He added that pushing the homosexual and forcing him to change can make his young life a misery and a torture.

There are other forms of sexual deviation — a term that simply means that sexual behavior is not carried on according to the "normal" accepted standard — but, once again, not everyone who behaves in a sexually unusual way is a degenerate. It also must be remembered that sexual behavior itself does not cause mental illness. It is our attitudes toward sex that touch off many emotional disorders, such as the guilt and anxiety many persons suffer over the performance of sexual acts and, in many cases, over the desire to perform such acts. Our sexual attitudes were shaped when we were very young, and far too often by single-minded parents who relied too heavily on church and clergy. While no one can dispute that both home and religion have much to offer in the way of positive sex education — provided they approach the subject as a normal and universal human experience — many times their treatment has been from a purely physical and biological standpoint. Often parents do talk about sex to their children, but in the wrong way. In an attempt to teach the child to be "normal," they recoil in horror at a scrawled obscenity on the side of a building, branding now common epithets as "dirty" and those who use them as "immoral," thereby heightening the natural curiosity of young people toward sex, and forcing them to equate meaningless shock phrases with "doing that nasty thing." Slowly, they begin to intertwine the meaning of sex with love — which, of course, it often is — but too frequently the term "making love" comes to mean "making out." Sex often does follow love (over the years, this pattern seems to have been more characteristic of women), and love can follow sex (more often in men, at least prior to women's sexual liberation), but the rule is not a hard and fast one. What is important is that we are all potentially sexual beings who are rightly interested in, and are shaped by, matters sexual, the self-righteous opponents of sex education and the self-appointed guardians of public morals notwithstanding.

Young people and many adults are caught between sexually provocative movies, television, advertisements, and books on the one hand and parental and religious messages of repression on the other. "The adolescent peer groups know that both are unrealistic, and in their groping they are repudiating society's placement of the erotic as the whole of sex," said Dr. Mary S. Calderone, one of the nation's leading exponents of sex education, at a Boston pediatricians' conference. "But just as realistically, they recognize that the sexual feelings and thoughts they have are a part of them that is impossible to repress."

There are many adults and young people who do not speak of sex at all, and this silence, too, has an important effect on later sexual behavior and attitudes. It can create as much guilt, frustration, and helplessness as the constant harping on sex as obscene. "Most parents do not communicate sexual information as much as anxiety," Professor John H. Gagnon, a sociologist at the State University of New York, told a 1969 colloquy on sexuality at

Michigan State University. At the same meeting, Dr. Albert Ellis, a New York psychotherapist and controversial expert on human sexuality, pointed out that literally millions of Americans, including untold numbers of college students, are still exceptionally guilty about sex in general and premarital affairs in particular. Such feeling is not healthy, he said, because guilt, when accurately defined, "is virtually always irrational, self-defeating and evil. In relation to sex behavior, it is particularly idiotic." Dr. Ellis said he found no fault with the rational element of guilt — that guilt which says, "I have done a wrong, erroneous, mistaken or unethical act, and it is unfortunate that I have committed this act." But he strongly rejected what he termed the irrational element in guilt — the conclusion that "because I unfortunately committed a wrong act, I am a pretty bad person." The latter feeling, he explained, usually encourages a person to put himself into a hell on earth and to stop progressive change.

Psychologists tell us that when sexuality is repressed, neurotic symptoms develop as substitutes, and that neuroses are inhibitions in the development of the sex drive, or libido. One of the most familiar repressed experiences is the Oedipus complex, which takes its name from Sophocles' play about a man who unintentionally marries his mother. The term has come to mean the abnormal attachment of a child to a parent of the opposite sex, and it surfaces in numerous cases of men who marry a mother image, if they ever find someone to measure up to that standard at all, and women who seek only a substitute father in a love relationship.

Repressed and poorly shaped attitudes toward sexuality have been blamed for a number of sexual deviations, but once again, it should be understood that traces of these may be found in many normal people. It is only when a person engages in some of these perversions to the exclusion of other ways of obtaining satisfaction that he can be regarded as a true sexual deviate. Voyeurism is one such perversion. The voyeur is the "Peeping Tom" who obtains his sexual gratification from watching others undress, or by staring at nudes or observing sexual acts. In exhibitionism, the person reveals his genital organs in what often is regarded as an attempt either to shock people he feels despise him or to demonstrate to himself and others that he is not sexually inadequate. The nymphomaniac is a female who has an abnormal desire for sexual intercourse and who is not satisfied no matter how many partners she chooses (the term should not be applied to persons who have a particularly active sex life). The nymphomaniac's male counterpart suffers from what is known as satyriasis. Both disorders may reflect unconscious homosexuality (because those so afflicted are unable to find satisfaction with members of the opposite sex). Or they may be marks of inferiority or guilt, which prevent them from obtaining satisfaction. Sadists derive sexual gratification from inflicting physical or psychological pain on others. They may be trying to prove that they are strong individuals. The sadist's opposite is the masochist, who gains his sexual pleasure from suffering, either self-inflicted or invited by others. The masochist may be a guilt-ridden individual who unconsciously welcomes punishment for his sins. Both sadism and masochism tend to coexist in the same person. Bestiality is sexual intercourse between a human and an animal, and it may be a sign of deep feelings of inferiority.

Some deviates rape, murder, and commit all sorts of

sexually aggressive acts on women and children. A sex murderer or a "sex maniac" commits his crimes in place of, or as part of, sexual relations. The "sex killer" is a particular type of psychotic personality, but though extremely dangerous, it is not common in the general or even the criminal population. "We do not have any complete understanding of such tragic behavior, but we do know that in many cases there has been an extremely disturbed family background and that they have suffered much in early life at the hands of violent, aggressive, depriving and depraved or psychotic parents," Dr. Donald Hayes Russell of the Boston University Law-Medicine Institute told a conference a few years ago. He added that many persons known for their aggressive activities or perversions may never commit a murder in the course of their lifetime.

It was noted earlier that sociopaths might make up the bulk of those we know as the mentally ill and that many of them do not get to hospitals. Of the individuals in institutions, however, there is little doubt that schizophrenia afflicts a huge portion of them, and that disorder will be examined next.

4 Schizophrenia

Sarah is nineteen years old and lives alone in an apartment in the city. She works as a secretary and is attractive, but has no steady boyfriend. In fact, she hardly dates at all, and only speaks when spoken to. Most of the time, Sarah seems reasonably normal. Her co-workers find her a bit strange, perhaps because she is so withdrawn, but most of them accept her as she is. A few others, turned off because she is somehow different, consider her "weird" or "spooky."

While Sarah is able to perform her routine office chores in a generally satisfactory way, there are times when it is not so easy. Often the world around her is transformed into a terrifying place. People and familiar objects seem to be like reflections in the distorting mirrors of a funhouse. The rhythmic snap of her electric typewriter's keys sometimes become as deafening as a street gang's jackhammer. The tuna sandwich that she usually enjoys at lunch takes on a loathsome taste. Even the smell of her perfume and the pleasant shaving lotion her boss wears sickens her. At night, it can be worse. She hears hissing voices, distant music, or a bumblebee's buzz. Her satin robe on the bed changes into a sinewy snake, and her bulky coat in the closet becomes a hulking bear. A television comedy brings her to tears; a tragedy causes her to laugh uncontrollably.

Understandably, Sarah is afraid. But the fear that engulfs her is not a rational one. She imagines her landlord is planning to kill her, and she hears him breathing outside her door when there is no one there. There are times when she is so tense she feels her head is about to spin off into space, and her mind is racing so fast she cannot brake it. Other times, her thoughts creep along at a maddeningly slow pace and, just as when they are running away, are disconnected. Were she to speak to someone, her words would make no sense whatsoever. She struggles to cool out her head, and she cannot, and the result, at the end of a long and sleepless night, is depression and fatigue.

Sarah doesn't know why her moods roller-coaster, or why her external world is often such a hideous nightmare.

Later, hopefully before it is too late, Sarah will see a psychiatrist, and he will diagnose her problem as schizophrenia, mankind's greatest mental crippler. A severe emotional disorder whose most important symptom is withdrawal from reality, schizophrenia afflicts between 2 and 3 million people in the United States and Canada. Those suffering from it fill nearly two-thirds of the beds in our mental institutions. Many thousands, however, are at large in the community, undiagnosed and uncared for. Each year, according to some estimates, between 100,000 and 300,000 new cases are discovered in the United States alone. Chances are that at least one family in your neighborhood has experienced the disease and another will suffer it later on. Although it can come on at any time, schizophrenia generally strikes younger men and women, roughly between the ages of fifteen and thirty-five. In fact, it was originally named *dementia praecox,* the Latin terms for madness and precocious, by Emil Kraepelin, the German "father of modern psychiatry," because it does develop in the early years. On a worldwide basis, one out of every hundred persons is, was, or will be afflicted with schizophrenia sometime in his life; the English writer, Aldous Huxley, once called it the plague of the twentieth century. The direct and indirect cost of this tragic disorder to victims, their families, and to taxpayers is huge, with estimates ranging around $4 billion a year — just about what alcoholism costs industry every year in lost manpower hours of production.

Schizophrenia is psychiatry's greatest challenge. Not only is it widespread, but it is quite difficult to cure. It can be controlled to some extent, but if left untreated it can force the victim to do violence to himself or to others. Its cause still baffles medical science, but both heredity and environment have been implicated.

Schizophrenia is Greek for "split mind." It does not mean that the schizophrenic's brain is divided into two parts, one good and the other evil. He is not a Dr. Jekyll turning into a Mr. Hyde and back again, although that popular analogy does describe the dual personality of the sufferer. The split is, in fact, between the schizophrenic and the real world. Preoccupied with nightmarish hallucinations, childish fantasies, and grandiose delusions, the schizophrenic retreats farther and farther from the everyday until only his body continues to live in society. His troubled mind, enveloped in a strange dream, is elsewhere.

There are many forms of schizophrenia, just as there are many kinds of cancer. Some psychiatrists believe it is not a single psychosis, but a whole group of psychoses with similar symptoms. There are four major types of schizophrenia: simple, hebephrenic, catatonic, and paranoid. In simple schizophrenia, the individual shows a lack of interest in life around him, and nothing, it seems, can turn him on. The hebephrenic pulls himself deeply into his shell, shunning the real world by giggling and engaging in silly behavior and childish mannerisms. The catatonic may literally freeze into position, a grin or a grimace fixed on his face. He may remain in this statuelike posture for several hours or for days, speechless and refusing food and drink. At other times, the catatonic flies into uncontrollable rage, to the point of attempting murder or suicide. The paranoid is defiant, disagreeable, and suspicious, and suffers from delusions. He may think he is Jesus or some world leader, or that someone is after him to do him harm. As far back as the second century A.D., Soranus of Ephesus, a Greek writer on medicine, told of people with delusions of grandeur who "believe themselves to be God." In this state, the schizophrenic may kill, turning his wrath on the person he is convinced is trying to do him in. Or, regarding himself as a divinely ordained executioner who answers an inner voice that commands him to rid the world of despots, he may murder an important person. One psychiatric study begun after the assassination of President Kennedy found that virtually all federal prisoners jailed for threatening the life of a president of the United States suffered from a severe form of schizophrenia. Lee Harvey Oswald, arrested for President

Kennedy's murder and himself murdered by Dallas night-club owner Jack Ruby, was diagnosed as showing a tendency toward schizophrenia in his youth.

Although the exact cause of schizophrenia remains a mystery, there are several intriguing theories that deal with it. The accepted one has been that it is a strictly psychological disorder arising from childhood disturbances and a bad family environment. Something is wrong between the child and his mother or father, or between the mother and father, and because of this adverse relationship the child's emotions and personality do not develop normally. He grows up with this flaw, and when a crisis hits — it can be as minor as who will do the dishes, or as shattering as a death — something gives way and he may become schizophrenic. The personality defect has made him vulnerable. So that he will not have to face a world that is bitter and painful to him, he hides in the world of illusion and delusion.

At a 1967 international conference on schizophrenia at the University of Rochester, a good deal of the analysis of the disease revolved around the influence of the family on the child's developing mind. One of the participants, Dr. Theodore Lidz, a professor of psychiatry at Yale University, stressed that man, unlike other animals, cannot rely on internal, instinctive information, but must learn from other human beings how to survive. Each individual's personality, and the adaptive techniques he acquires, can be more or less tailored to the environment, social system, and culture in which he happens to be reared. "It is a vastly different mechanism for survival and adaptation from that possessed by other animals, and unless we take full cognizance of it, we can never understand human functioning properly," he added.

At the same symposium, Dr. Don Jackson, director of the Mental Research Institute of Palo Alto, California, also emphasized the child's need for vital information from his parents. He pointed out that this need makes the child vulnerable to mental disturbances if the messages he receives from his parents are contradictory or conflict with the information he receives from the rest of society.

If the environment is to blame, then, say some researchers, changing it during childhood may help. One Boston study of the life histories of schizophrenics led the investigators to conclude that a friendship with a teacher or doctor, admission to a different school, or a change in the home environment during childhood may have kept some adults from contracting the illness. These "saving events" may have helped lift the stress under which some emotionally disturbed children might have become schizophrenic.

Twins, which occur about once in every eighty-six pregnancies, are fairly good human laboratories for behavioral studies. There are two classes of twins. Fraternal twins, which develop from two eggs fertilized by separate sperm, are no more similar than other children in the same family. Identical twins, who are about a third as common as fraternal twins, come from one egg fertilized by one sperm. Identical twins are always of the same sex and have exactly the same color hair and eyes. They are, in effect, carbon copies of each other.

Environmental factors emerged as paramount in another study, this one involving more than three hundred pairs of schizophrenic twins in Norway. It was demonstrated that although schizophrenia was more often found in two identical twins than in fraternal twins, the difference in incidence was not as great as had been reported earlier. Both American and European studies have shown that if one identical twin developed schizophrenia, chances are that the other would, too. The Norwegian group found that schizophrenia in both members of a pair of idential twins occurred in between 25 and 38 percent of all cases. After the researchers analyzed their data, they found that when both twins became schizophrenic they apparently had had to contend with more childhood stresses. They also were locked within their families, were close to each other, and, therefore, had little opportunity to develop individually or be influenced by outsiders.

While it has long been held that there is always something seriously wrong with a schizophrenic's family environment, more and more attention now is being paid to the theory that schizophrenia is a physical disease, just as diabetes is a physical disease. In fact, many scientists believe that an error in the body's chemistry, probably inherited, is at the root of the problem.

Disease, of course, can have many different causes, both direct and predisposing causes. Among the direct causes are such things as germs and viruses, poor nutrition, toxic chemicals such as the lead in paints, mercury accumulation in fish, and various pesticides. There is the polluting smoke from industrial stacks as well as the harmful effects of cigarette smoking. Other direct causes of disease include neoplasms, new growths such as cancers and tumors, and a number of degenerative, or aging, processes. Birth defects can be a cause of disease, and are either inherited or congenital. Inherited disorders are passed on through the genes from parent to offspring, such as the blood disorder hemophilia (bleeder's disease), which is transmitted by females, who are not generally affected by it, to male offspring. Congenital defects, such as cleft palate and harelip, are usually acquired during the developmental stages in the womb, and may or may not be related to any hereditary influence.

The terms inherited and congenital are often confused. Congenital means "born with," and implies that heredity has nothing to do with the problems that arise. But the birth of a baby is not the beginning of his or her life, for that started long before, when sperm and egg united. Congenital defects, then, *could* be the result of something gone wrong in the reproductive cells of the parents, as well as the result of direct injury to the fetus. The term inborn (natural) always implies a hereditary influence, and an inborn defect or quality may be called congenital. On the other hand, a congenital defect is not necessarily inborn.

Predisposing causes, such as age and sex, are those that do not directly cause a disease. They boost the chances, however, of a person's becoming ill. Males, for example, are more prone to heart disease and ulcers than women; children have a better chance than adults of contracting measles and rheumatic fever; women are more apt to get gallbladder disease than men; diabetes is more common in people over forty.

Some people inherit a tendency toward certain diseases, as opposed to actually inheriting a disorder. These people start life with a built-in weakness of some sort that makes them susceptible to a disease. For instance, people don't inherit allergies such as hay fever. They may, however, develop the predisposition, or tendency, to become allergic. If both parents are allergic, or if there is allergy on both sides of the family, chances are the children will develop an allergy. Diabetes, a disorder in which the body fails to use sugar properly, is also usually due to an inherited tendency.

In viewing schizophrenia as a physical disease, both direct and predisposing causes come into play. Heredity, chemicals, and brain defects are all under consideration by those seeking to solve the riddle, for it has been said that "to know schizophrenia is to know psychiatry."

Hereditary studies of schizophrenia have been underway for many years, and many authorities believe strongly that there must be certain inherent predisposing flaws present if the disease is to appear. Some years ago Dr. Franz J. Kallmann, a professor of psychiatry at Columbia University, established that if one of two identical twins is schizophrenic there was an 85 percent chance that the other would be, and a 13 percent chance that he would be schizoid, a term that describes the traits of shyness and introversion — which are seen, of course, in an exaggerated form in schizophrenia itself. Dr. Kallmann and others also found that if a child has a schizophrenic mother or father he has a 16 percent chance of having the same disorder and a 32 percent chance of being schizoid. If both parents are schizophrenic, the child has a 68 percent chance of having the disease.

Twin studies, while they are valuable, are marred by one important factor, which is that twins are almost always raised in the same home. They share the same environment and are hardly ever raised apart, making it most difficult to separate nature from nurture. Identical twins are also usually treated more alike than fraternal twins, a fact that makes researchers wonder if the schizophrenia that shows up in them is more psychological than genetic.

Because of this difficulty, those interested in the genetic aspects of the disorder have been looking closely at the adopted-away children of schizophrenic parents. Some of the studies have yielded striking evidence that heredity is an important factor that cannot be ignored. They have demonstrated that if a child is taken away from its schizophrenic mother shortly after birth and given up for adoption to a well-adjusted couple, the child develops schizophrenia anyway. One study of 47 children born to schizophrenic mothers and separated permanently from them shortly after birth revealed that five of the offspring had schizophrenia. Half of them also had what the investigators called major psychosocial disabilities; some were diagnosed as sociopathic, others as neurotic, and a few as mentally deficient, with I.Q.s of less than 70 (the average is 100).

In another study, researchers looked at 39 children of schizophrenic parents who were adopted by normal persons before they were a year old and compared these children with 47 children of normal parents who also were adopted by normal families. Of the 39 whose parents were schizophrenic, 13 became either schizophrenic or schizoid. Only seven of the 47 children whose parents were normal, on the other hand, had any kind of mental disorder. The study, conducted by the National Institute of Mental Health, found also that the children of normal parents who were mentally ill were not as sick as the children whose parents were schizophrenic. Because more mental illness occurred in the group of children whose natural parents were schizophrenic, and because both groups studied were raised by normal persons, the government researchers concluded that heredity had to be at work.

These studies do not mean that upbringing can be discounted in the quest for a cause of schizophrenia, or that people who have parents free of the disease will not get it. A good many of the investigators of heredity feel that upbringing may be extremely important, and that no matter what the cause, it is strengthened by frightening and domineering treatment — even neglect — of a child during his growing years. They see the disease as caused by a combination of genetic and environmental factors, pointing to the fact that the severity of the illness is less when the child of schizophrenic parents is raised in an adoptive home. A study conducted by Dr. Seymour S. Kety, a professor of psychiatry at Harvard Medical School, raised the possibility recently that adoption, in fact, might be a good thing for the children of schizophrenics. If schizophrenia depends on both an environmental and a genetic factor, he explained, then in the natural families of schizophrenics both are at work. The odds change, however, if one takes a person born of a family with a genetic predisposition to the disease and transplants him to another family at random. "The chances that the adopting family will have the environmental factors necessary for schizophrenia are no greater than the chances of any household at random having them," Dr. Kety believes. "Transplanting him, should, therefore, diminish the risk if our preliminary findings are proved."

As matters now stand, and probably will for years to come, scientists searching for the actual genes that cause the disease or a predisposition to it have no easy task. The various shapes that schizophrenia takes, coupled with the fact that environment always hovers outside the laboratory door, are roadblocks to any simple "Eureka, I've found it" kind of discovery. Several years ago, government scientists studied the first recorded case of identical quadruplets who had schizophrenia. Their investigation turned up evidence that a defective gene might have passed on the tendency toward the disorder, and that the girls' father came from a family with a history of mental illness. The quads and their father also had similar abnormal brain waves. But the investigators also found that serious environmental problems plagued the family. They concluded that while in most cases an inherited defect must be present for the disease to break out, without severe environmental pressure it might not appear, even in those predisposed to it. Dr. Kety, whose group believes that a personality type vulnerable to schizophrenia, and not schizophrenia itself, is passed on genetically, maintains that whether a person becomes schizophrenic depends on what life situation he meets and what environment he faces. He also cites evidence from other studies that creativity seems to run high in the families of schizophrenics. It thus may well be that the same genetic trait that produces schizophrenia in one person produces creativity in another, depending on other genetic factors and environment.

What cannot be overlooked amid all of this interaction between heredity and environment is the simple fact that often, whenever an inherited defect appears, so too does some foulup in the body's chemical makeup. And it is in this biochemical area of research that some of the most exciting leads in the genetics of schizophrenia are being pursued. So important is this avenue of investigation that a group of distinguished scientists formed the American Schizophrenia Foundation a few years ago to seek the cure and treatment of the disease by studying its biochemical and genetic causes.

Proponents of the biochemical theory — that schizophrenia is basically an inherited chemical defect — point to the fact that many disorders are caused by such abnormalities. One is PKU, or phenylketonuria, a defect in the body's chemistry that prevents assimilation of amino acids (the building blocks of proteins), found in most protein-rich foods. This defect eventually causes mental retardation. In the schizophrenic, the defect is said to produce poisonous substances that affect the brain much as overdoses of drugs or alcohol do, creating marked disturbances in perception and drastic changes in thought, personality, and behavior. These abnormal chemicals have been found in the blood, urine, and tissues of those afflicted with the disorder. When they are injected into the bloodstreams of laboratory animals or normal persons, they create many of the classic symptoms of schizophrenia.

As far back as 1941, a professor of biochemistry at Northwestern University, Dr. E. Albert Zeller, discovered that there was a significantly high level of the enzyme monoamine oxidase (MO) in the brains of schizophrenics. Enzymes are complicated chemical structures with jaw-breaking names, and there are more than 100,000 of them in each cell in our bodies. The biochemical "middlemen" of the body's chemistry, they affect just about everything you are and everything you do. They are the sparks of life, chemical workhorses that speed up the thousands of changes that take place continuously in our bodies. Without them, food would go undigested, tissue would not be built, and blood cells would not be replaced. With no enzyme action you would not be able to read or understand the words on this page, scratch your head, or draw a breath. It has been said that whenever a gene wants something done, it produces a specific enzyme to do the job. At the same time, when something goes wrong with a gene, something also happens to the enzyme it is supposed to produce. It may be missing or warped or there may be too much of it. And disease may result.

Around the time Dr. Zeller was studying the MO enzyme, another scientist, Dr. Albert Hofmann, made another discovery that would affect Dr. Zeller's work. Working in his laboratory, Dr. Hofmann tasted lysergic acid diethylamide, that most powerful member of the so-called hallucinogen family now popularly known as LSD. Later, he began to have hallucinations. He continued experimenting, and concluded that LSD produced symptoms much like those found in schizophrenics. A person "tripping" on LSD experiences marked changes in sensation. Time, for example, seems to race, stop, slow down, or run backward. The user sees strange shapes and patterns, his sensitivity to sound increases, food may feel gritty in his mouth, and he may hear voices and music. He may feel he is separated from his body, from the real world, and he may have delusions. His emotions run the gamut from pure ecstasy to utter horror. One of the most confusing reactions is the sense of two strong and opposite feelings at the same time. The user can be happy and sad at the same moment, or relaxed and tense. While there is some question whether LSD itself can cause mental illness in a previously stable individual, there is little doubt that the drug can help bring about acute and sometimes long-lasting mental illness in people prone to such a disorder. Too often, it is such people who are most attracted to LSD in the hope it will expand their minds and make them more creative.

After Dr. Hofmann's discovery, researchers found that

LSD seems to affect the levels of certain chemicals in the brain, like serotonin, a hormonelike substance that may influence nervous system activity. Animal experiments with LSD suggested that when the animal ingested the drug its brain's normal filtering and screening-out process became blocked, causing it to become flooded with un-selected sights and sounds — an overload of stimulation to the senses.

Researchers had also found that the brains of schizo-phrenics seemed to have a deficiency of serotonin. Because Dr. Zeller discovered that there was also a high level of the MO enzyme in their brains, it was logically concluded that the enzyme was a serotonin-destroyer. Experimenting with a drug called iproniazid, Dr. Zeller found that it stopped MO from knocking out the sero-tonin. Using the drug, and another to restore normal amounts of serotonin to the brain, he was able to achieve some favorable results in a number of psychotic patients he treated.

More recently, Canadian resarchers identified different colored "spots" in the urine of LSD users as the same chemical found in studies with psychotic patients. The compound, known as kryptopyrrole, is found nowhere else in nature, and though it has been found in various forms in both LSD users and psychotic patients, its source is unknown.

In 1957, scientists at Tulane University, led by Dr. Robert Heath, made another significant discovery that lent a good deal of support to the proponents of schizo-phrenia's biochemical origins. They found a strange sub-stance in the blood of schizophrenics that, when injected into monkeys, caused changes in brain waves very much like those found in schizophrenics. When the substance, named taraxein, was given to human volunteers who were not schizophrenics, they too developed schizophrenic behavior.

Ten years later, Dr. Heath suggested that schizophrenia may be what scientists call an autoimmune disease, one in which antibodies, the body's disease-fighters, mistakenly attack normal cells. Usually our antibodies are our natural defense against invading disease-causing substances, known as antigens. The antibody-antigen reaction is best observed when tissues are assailed by bacteria through a wound in the skin. The body immediately mobilizes teams of specialized cells and sends them to the wound. Some of these cells wrap themselves around the invaders, recognizing them as "not self," and sap them of strength with digestive enzymes.

But sometimes this well-organized defense system doesn't work as it should. For some strange reason the body turns on itself, as it were, makes antibodies against its own tissues, and in the process causes a variety of diseases, among which may be rheumatoid arthritis, hepatitis, and some forms of anemia.

According to Dr. Heath, taraxein may be an antibody produced by the body and directed against specific areas of brain tissue where certain changes tied to schizophrenia occur. If all of this is true, it may be possible to create a neutralizing agent to fight the schizophrenia antibodies, and the prospect for a chemical treatment of the disorder may be bright indeed.

In another laboratory study of schizophrenia-linked chemicals at the Worcester Foundation for Experimental Biology in Massachusetts, rats that had been trained to climb ropes were injected with a complex substance found in traces in all human blood but more so in schizophrenics. Fifteen minutes after the injection, the rats became disoriented, climbed the rope haltingly, gazed about in confusion, and sometimes never reached the food reward at the top. Some slipped listlessly to the floor, or spun dizzily down the rope.

Other investigators have suggested that many schizophrenics have an abnormal amount of a normal blood substance. This excess appears to weaken the membranes of nerve and other cells, forcing vital chemicals to leak into and out of the cells. This might injure the cells badly enough to start the symptoms of schizophrenia. It has also been proposed that the disease may be caused by diets lacking in zinc and high in copper. Metal trace elements find their way into our bodies through the soil and water, in the vegetables and meat and fish we eat, and in the water we drink. Many of them are essential to growth and survival, others are harmful. And in excessive amounts even those good for us may be bad. So it is with zinc and copper, both of which may cause deficiency disease or have a beneficial effect, depending on the amounts ingested. In schizophrenia, according to one recent report, the low zinc, high copper diet was responsible for the disorder in some 80 percent of 250 schizophrenic patients studied over three years. The metal imbalance, it is believed, stems from the fact that drinking water comes to us mainly through copper pipes, whereas in the past the pipes were galvanized — iron coated with zinc. Since a number of enzyme actions are dependent on the right balance of trace metals, in schizophrenia, presumably, the brain is overstimulated when the enzyme action is flawed.

In the study, all the patients with the metal imbalance reportedly improved after taking extra zinc and removing copper from their diets.

And so the laboratory data continue to grow, and with them the hope that schizophrenia will not only be cured but also prevented. "Before anyone can get schizophrenia," according to two psychiatric researchers, Dr. Abram Hoffer and Dr. Humphrey Osmond, "his body 'factory' must be different from that of a normal subject in that it must have the capacity to go out of order for some reason, and start biochemical changes in motion. This is an essential cause of schizophrenia. Without it, the disease cannot occur. With it, it may occur, but it also may not, just as everyone susceptible to tuberculosis does not develop tuberculosis."

The biochemical case for schizophrenia is, then, a strong one, summed up this way by the American Schizophrenia Foundation: "Negative emotional factors — like fear and hatred, despair and self-pity — can trigger or aggravate the condition, but the underlying physiological weakness is the basic cause."

Given all the factors that may be blamed for schizophrenia, natural or nurtured, is there a best way to treat the disease? Just how much hope for a cure can a schizophrenic have?

There is, of course, no simple solution, mostly because of the many variables that surround the disorder. Just as there is disagreement over what causes it, so, too, there is a wide difference of opinion over how best to treat it. Some schizophrenics are given shock therapy, a form of psychiatric treatment in which an electrical current or insulin, a hormone that controls our blood sugar level, is administered to the patient. The resulting convulsions sometimes help to favorably shift the disorder's course. Surgical treatment may be decided upon, specifically a technique known as a lobotomy. A neurosurgeon cuts into portions of the brain and removes certain areas in an effort to alter its functions, and, it is hoped, to put behavior back on the right track. Psychosurgery, as this approach is sometimes called, is controversial, however, just as shock therapy is, and many psychiatrists see it as a last resort in schizophrenia.

Psychoanalysis may be used, but in the last few years many analysts have been following the advice of Sigmund Freud that schizophrenia does not respond to such treatment, and that analysis is more of a diagnostic tool than a method of treating psychoses. "It is of the utmost importance to recognize the early presence of the disease," Dr. Heath has warned, because the therapist who does not "may undertake a kind of psychotherapy that can result in dire consequences." In this matter of the psychiatric approach, the controversial Scotch-born psychiatrist, Dr. Ronald D. Laing, has objected to calling schizophrenia a disease in the ordinary sense. At the Rochester conference mentioned earlier, Dr. Laing — who has aroused the ire of his peers by questioning society's sanity and by suggesting that individual madness was but a reflection of that society's ills and evils — preferred to call schizophrenia a "breakdown in interpersonal relationships." He has stressed the need for establishing a close-knit familylike situation in which to work with these individuals, and has argued that the psychiatrist must understand what the schizophrenic's "real world" is rather than impose another version of reality on him. At Kingsley Hall, a commune

for schizophrenics he helped found, Dr. Laing was so successful with his patients that only a few of the sixty-five
had to be hospitalized later. In that setting, psychiatrists
and nonprofessional workers lived with the schizophrenics, with no boundary between "insane" patients and
"normal" doctors. Coupling this personal atmosphere
with a variety of therapies, including painting, poetry
reading, dancing, and movies, the schizophrenics' shattered relationships with others were built up.

This kind of communal therapy, which does away with
the traditional doctor-patient relationship, has been
employed successfully by a number of other groups. In
one experiment conducted a few years ago by a Harvard
team, a previously locked ward of hard-core schizophrenic patients in a private psychiatric hospital responded so
well to regular get-togethers in a large hall that several
got jobs outside the hospital. The entire group often went
bowling or to a club for dancing and dinner, and many
began contributing constructively to the hospital and
relating to the community for the first time in twenty or
thirty years. In another study, of 200 schizophrenics in
Louisville, Kentucky, it was demonstrated that schizophrenic patients do much better with home care than in
the hospital. The doctor who made the study believed
that if a disease as severe as schizophrenia could be
treated in the community, there was no reason why other
problems — such as mental retardation, alcoholism, drug
addiction, and senility — could not be handled in like
fashion.

Another way to treat schizophrenia is with medication,
and some psychiatrists rely heavily on tranquilizers, anti-
depressants, and even vitamins. But many physicians and

lay people feel strongly that we have become too dependent on drugs as a substitute for human care. As an example, they cite the use of methadone, an addictive drug, to help heroin addicts kick the habit. Those who oppose this substitution of one addictive habit for another argue that it is one more "easy way out," an admission of defeat, that it is the same as taking an alcoholic off whiskey and giving him gin, and that the self-help approach — in which addicts go "cold turkey" and remain off heroin with the assistance of ex-addicts — is best because it faces up to the problem. Treating schizophrenics with drugs, they say, merely suppresses the disease's symptoms and doesn't really help the sufferer face up to his illness. One recent study, in fact, found that some patients may even do better without tranquilizers. Certain types of schizophrenics — those who are not paranoid and who had been socially well adjusted before they became ill — showed more symptoms of illness on a tranquilizer regimen than did similar patients treated with a placebo (an inactive substance, such as a sugar pill, given to satisfy a patient's demand for medicine). The researchers who conducted the government-sponsored study reported that the positive behavioral changes in patients given the placebo — some of whom had shorter hospital stays than those on the drugs — apparently resulted from the effects of a beneficial hospital environment.

Nevertheless, drug therapy has an important place in schizophrenia, either alone or in combination with psychotherapy and communal therapy, and for every report that it does little to help there is one calling attention to dramatic improvement in medicated patients. Some of the drugs have an obvious calming effect on the patients and, while they do not seem to bring about any lasting or fundamental change in the disease itself, they do improve behavior. Others appear to have an antischizophrenic effect; that is, they seem to be able to get at the root of the disease. One analogy to show the effect of drugs might be the use of aspirin to treat arthritics. For years it was prescribed for the pain that accompanies the disorder, but researchers have discovered that it also has an effect on the inflammation that is the disease's hallmark.

A study at the Massachusetts Mental Health Center not too long ago demonstrated that two years of psychotherapy unsupported by drug therapy does little or nothing for the chronic schizophrenic. In the survey, all patients received intensive individual psychotherapy, but only half the patients in each group got a tranquilizer, the others being given a placebo. According to the doctors, the patients on the drug, though still ill, changed noticeably. One still heard voices but he no longer shouted at the physicians or did cartwheels in response to their commands, as he had before. He appeared to be more normal, and people were able to relate to him in a more reasonable way. He was also able to leave the hospital for short periods of time to work. On the other hand, the patients who had received psychotherapy and the placebo did not appear to change over the two years. It was the psychiatrists' conclusion that, while long-term psychotherapy is of doubtful value, the tranquilizer treatment was perhaps one of the most useful tools available for the management of chronic schizophrenic patients. Other studies have come up with similar positive results and, according to a recent report from the National Institute of Mental Health, the major tranquilizers must be given major credit for the 30 percent decline in the number of patients hospitalized with schizophrenia, a drop that has taken place since the drugs were introduced some fifteen years ago.

Vitamin therapy, a somewhat controversial method, is also being tried by several investigators who are using massive doses of vitamins to treat not only schizophrenia and autism, a form of childhood schizophrenia characterized by complete withdrawal, but also such disorders as alcoholism and senility. Many of those who oppose this megavitamin therapy offer basically the same reasons as those who are against heavy reliance on drugs. But they also see a danger in people putting blind faith in an experimental Pied Piper to the exclusion of other forms of treatment. Since hospitalization is most important for schizophrenics who are suicidal or abusive, to delay hospitalization at the urging of someone who has heard of the miracles wrought by vitamin therapy would be disastrous.

Dr. Hoffer and Dr. Osmond began treating schizophrenic patients with vitamin B_3 (also called niacin and nicotinic acid) in 1952 after a series of trials that produced excellent results. In 1971, at a conference of the Canadian and American Schizophrenia associations and the Schizophrenia Association of Great Britain, Dr. Hoffer expressed the opinion that a daily dose of B_3 for everyone might reduce the incidence of schizophrenia. Noting that he believed the disorder is marked by a relative deficiency of the vitamin, Dr. Hoffer declared: "Certain people require much more [vitamin B_3] than is provided in the diet. If we were to add to our diet at least one gram a day, we could, in the next decade or two, see a very significant decrease in the extent of this disease."

Citing case records of the results of using vitamins in 2,000 patients, he said he had had a better than 90 percent recovery rate with schizophrenics who had been ill for a year or less. The condition of the remaining 10 percent improved. Along the same line, another physician, in New York, reported recently that he had treated 5,000 schizophrenic patients with huge doses of vitamins and had had improvement in more than 4,000. He used the vitamins as a supplement to psychotherapy and drug therapy and was able to cut their rehospitalization rate in half, just about stop suicides, and double the recovery rate.

Chemist Linus Pauling, the only man to win two Nobel prizes and widely known for his belief that ascorbic acid (vitamin C) can prevent colds, also believes that vitamins can help cure mental illness. "I believe that mental disease is, for the most part, caused by abnormal [chemical] reaction rates," Dr. Pauling has said, "and by abnormal molecular concentrations of essential substances. Significant improvements in the mental health of many persons might be achieved by the provision of the optimum molecular concentrations of substances normally present in the human body." He feels that vitamin therapy is better than other methods of treatment because it does involve the use of natural substances already in the body.

In the July 18, 1973, issue of *Psychiatric News*, the official newspaper of the American Psychiatric Association, an APA expert task force challenged megavitamin therapy in the treatment of schizophrenia and deplored the publicity it has been given. In its first formal position on the matter, the APA task force said that the theoretical basis for megavitamin treatment, especially with nicotinic acid, has been "found wanting" and that results of serious and major attempts to demonstrate the value of nicotinic acid have been "uniformly negative."

It should be obvious by now that schizophrenia researchers have not yet been completely successful in their quest for a cure. Until it can be definitely established that the disease is behavioral or chemical or a combination of the two, there will be differences of opinion on how best to treat it.

Some of the approaches described give reason for optimism, however, and it must be emphasized again that many people suffering from schizophrenia have returned to work and are living relatively well in their communities. It must also be stressed that quick diagnosis is the first important step in treating any disorder. If schizophrenia is not identified promptly and if treatment is not begun at an early age, the consequences may well be catastrophic, since long-standing schizophrenia does not respond well to treatment.

Above all, the schizophrenic must be looked upon as the human being that he is, not as some shameful creature to be hidden in a closet. Too often, we shrink away when mental illness strikes a relative or friend. We are afraid of it, and we consider the sufferer an embarrassment. Such a Dark Ages attitude must change. For it is only with the help of an enlightened public, willing to face mental illness openly as an illness and not as a curse, that schizophrenia and other disorders of the mind will be conquered. Sympathy, understanding, and patience are prime requisites. Laboratories can do little for schizophrenia if there is no money, public or private, to pay for research. Neither can hospitals or mental health clinics continue to function without financial aid. Funds go to popular causes, and until the public cares enough about mental illness little will be accomplished.

5 Retardation

Not so many years ago, the term "feeble-minded" was widely used to describe unfortunate people whose mental development seemed to have stopped. The word could be found in medical textbooks as well as in popular reading material, and the general assumption was that one so afflicted was lacking in intelligence, as one scientific treatise put it, or was simply an "idiot," as another defined him.

Today, fortunately, the term is obsolete in medical circles, for it carries with it the erroneous implication that nothing can be done to help one born with such a problem. "Feeble-mindedness" has given way to the term "mental retardation," which, according to the American Association of Mental Deficiency, is "sub-average intellectual functioning which originates during the development period."

While the attitudes toward mental retardation have changed markedly over the past few years, traces of past ignorance linger. Myths die hard. They cling to life like patches of snow in the springtime, and some individuals — you may know some among your own friends and family — unwilling to learn new truths, callously preserve and pass along fallacious ideas. The retarded are treated by such people as court jesters and freaks. This is tragic, for the retarded are handicapped, just as the blind are, and ridiculing and refusing to help them is akin to kicking a sightless person's cane from under him, or not lending him a hand to board a bus.

"Mental retardation," said President John F. Kennedy, one of whose sisters is retarded, "ranks as a major national health, social and economic problem. It strikes our most precious asset, our children."

What is this condition that afflicts more than 5 million Americans, that strikes 126,000 newborns a year and countless others who are able to limp along, undiagnosed as deficient? Part of the answer lies in what mental retardation is not. It isn't, as so many believe, a mental illness, a sickness. Mental illness, as we have seen thus far, has to do with an upset of the emotions or personality. The mentally retarded are not ill in that sense. A child so affected merely learns at a slower pace than the normal child and doesn't absorb the same amount of knowledge. But the retardate can learn, and he does. His problem is that his mental development is impaired or incomplete. Teaching him can be a little like filling a bottle through a narrow funnel that clogs and stops the flow every so often. How much eventually finds its way into the bottle, and how fast, depends on the size of the funnel opening and the consistency of the liquid poured in. The retardate learns, but how much depends on the amount and kind of effort that is made.

The measure of intelligence is the I.Q., with a measurement of 100 being the average. An I.Q. of 50 to 70 signals mild retardation; 35 to 49 is moderate; 20 to 34 is severe; and below 20 is profound. These measures also identify three levels of mental deficiency, terms that are used quite loosely in daily conversation with no regard for the seriousness of the states they describe — idiot, imbecile, and moron. An idiot is at the bottom of the scale, with a mental age of less than three years when adult and an I.Q. of less than 20. Idiots, who represent only about 5 percent of mental defectives, are obviously grossly retarded. They cannot be trained, though some learn simple duties, among them proper toilet habits. Totally dependent, they require nursing care, cannot learn to dress or bathe; speak only a few words, and understand commands only if they are direct and uncomplicated. Physically, many idiots are weakened individuals. They cannot stand or even sit up, and in an action characteristic of their state, roll their heads back and forth. Some speak loudly and are given to fits of rage and destructiveness; others, like the catatonic schizophrenic described in the previous chapter, remain immobile, a vacant stare on their faces. There is a separate category called idiot savant, which refers to a mental defective who is able to perform a number of remarkable feats in one direction, such as calendar calculation or puzzle solving.

Imbeciles, who represent some 20 percent of the defective population, have a mental age between three and seven and an I.Q. between 25 and 50 on some scales, between 20 and 49 on others. With an intelligence greater than that of the idiot but less than the moron's, imbeciles fall into the moderately retarded category. (Some list moderate as between 35 and 50.) They are generally able to guard themselves against common physical dangers, something the idiot cannot do, and are trainable to some extent. Some upper-level imbeciles learn to read primer-like words and can be taught to care for themselves and do simple chores. But it is unlikely that they can earn a living on their own. Imbeciles have been described as generally extremely affectionate and agreeable.

Morons, classified under mildly retarded, have an I.Q. between 50 and 70 and are usually incapable of developing beyond a mental age of eight to twelve. They are educable, however, can learn academic skills up to about the sixth grade level, and can often learn to perform a number of jobs to help support themselves. They may need guidance and assistance under unusual social or economic stress and, because they are vulnerable and respond to suggestion, are prey to some unsavory individuals who occasionally train them to commit criminal acts.

While the terms idiot, imbecile, and moron are still used in parts of Europe, they are generally looked upon with disfavor in the United States, and are obsolete for the most part. The preferred classifications for retardates are mild, moderate, severe, and profound. And it is under the first of these, the mildly deficient, all educable, that 85 percent of the cases fall. Another 10 to 12 percent are trainable, leaving only a relative handful who require permanent hospitalization. (Even severe cases of mental retardation can be taught to some extent, enough at least for them to communicate and care for themselves under supervision.) Insofar as the few profoundly affected are concerned, they remain human beings who need love and affection, even though they are totally dependent.

One might get the impression from these measurements and classifications that defining mental retardation is a fairly simple matter and that each case fits neatly into its own numbered pigeonhole. That is not so, however. First of all, there is little agreement among scientists and educators as to what intelligence itself actually is. In contrast to instinct — the inborn drives such as self-preservation — intelligence is defined in the American Psychiatric Association's standard glossary as "the potential ability of an individual to understand what he needs to recall and to mobilize and integrate constructively previous learning and experience in meeting new situations." In its lowest terms, intelligence may be said to be present when an animal or human being is at all aware of the relevance of his behavior to some objective. Intelligence has also been defined as the ability to meet unique situations or to learn to do so by new adaptive responses, and the ability to perform tests or tasks involving the grasping of relationships, "the degree of intelligence being proportional to the complexity or the abstractness or both of the relationships."

The tests employed to measure intelligence have also come under fire. Many scientists feel that they monitor a limited range of mental qualities and that they do not measure what may be termed absolute, native intelligence. They believe that a number of factors, such as environment and level of education, have to be considered when comparing intelligence test scores. Take, for instance, a poorly educated individual from a ghetto environment. He scores badly on an I.Q. test. Later he is retrained. If he does much better on a retesting (something that has happened time and again), he is then qualified to do the job that his original low I.Q. would have prevented him from doing. Critics of I.Q. tests also charge that the tests are generally based on what white, middle-class children can achieve and that they are, therefore, biased against other racial groups or poor whites. If this is true, then the differences that have been noted between test scores of blacks and whites might be a reflection of the original test bias. Others disagree, notably Dr. Arthur Jensen, a psychologist at the University of California. In 1969, he published a paper reporting that the reason blacks scored lower than whites on such tests was a lower I.Q. that was inherited, not conditioned by a poor environment. Others, also on the side of the genes, have concluded that I.Q. is about 85 percent heredity, about the same percentage of inheritance linked to body build.

I.Q. tests, it should be emphasized, are not foolproof, and while they help to measure levels of intelligence — whatever they may be — they are by no means the last word. (Consider the case of the aforementioned idiot savant.) The I.Q. is no precise measure of a person's value or potential, and to rely solely on test results when shaping a treatment program for the retarded does a disservice to the person afflicted.

The term mental retardation itself is a rather ambiguous and relative one. Even health professionals have a difficult time defining what they mean by it. In fact, a recent survey of Boston nurses disclosed that not one was able to define mental retardation adequately. Nurses Gladys M. Scipien of Boston University School of Nursing and Marie Wildoner of the Catherine Laboure School of Nursing polled ten nurses in a pediatric hospital and ten in a maternity hospital, both affiliated with the same medical center. In general, all twenty responses indicated an inability to define mental retardation adequately. Some of the answers were "slow learner," a "special child," a "person unable to cope with society," a "child with a low I.Q.," and a "child whose mental abilities are not equal to his chronological age." The lack of knowledge regarding the degree of retardation, the nurses said, was evidenced by one respondent who said that a retarded person was one "who could be trained, but could not be educated."

What causes this deficiency that affects some 3 percent of our population?

Again there is no one factor to blame, just as there is no single cause of schizophrenia or cancer or heart disease. There are hundreds of kinds of mental retardation, and science has been able to identify a cause in only about a quarter of them. Wayward genes, viruses, enzyme deficiency, brain injuries and infections before birth, medication, malnutrition and lack of nutrition, heavy metal poisoning, poor environment, lack of opportunity, no family cohesion, stifled initiative – all have been implicated. Here are nature and nurture again, often hopelessly intertwined, but every so often split apart long enough for researchers to focus on one or the other with promising results.

It is difficult to say which area of research is or will be the most fruitful. But certainly there has been heightened interest over the past few years in the biochemical possibilities. Just as in the case of schizophrenia, genetically determined defects – what scientists refer to as inborn errors of metabolism – have held the research spotlight. And if causes continue to be found – as they are, slowly but surely – the implications for the whole field of mental illness are obvious.

If anything is to blame for these inborn errors of

metabolism, it probably is an enzyme deficiency, and a good deal of the research is aimed at discovering which of these chemical workhorses is guilty. In the discussion of schizophrenia, it was noted that whenever a gene wants something done, it produces a specific enzyme to do the job, and that when something goes amiss with a gene something also happens to the enzyme it is supposed to produce, and disease results.

One of the most intensely studied deficiencies based on a metabolic flaw was mentioned earlier, PKU. Discovered in 1934, the disorder begins at birth and affects between one in 10,000 and one in 20,000. There is compelling evidence that it nearly always results in mental retardation unless the individual is placed on a special diet during his first months of life. PKU results in the inability to convert an amino acid called phenylalanine into tyrosine, another essential building block, due to a genetic enzyme defect. Thus thwarted, phenylalanine in the blood breaks down into phenylpyruvic acid, which affects the brain by interfering with its development and thus causing mental retardation. (Phenylalanine is one of the essential amino acids of protein, and makes up about 5 percent of all food protein.) PKU can be detected in infancy by testing the urine for the presence of phenylpyruvic acid. Many states now require that infants be tested for PKU at birth in order that proper treatment can be initiated before they become retarded. Interestingly, biochemical symptoms similar to those seen in PKU have been observed in fish after long-term exposure to a persistent pesticide called dieldrin that has been found in 93 percent of freshwater fish in a national study. Dr. Paul Mehrle, a researcher with the U.S. Department of the Interior in Missouri, told a meeting of the American Chemical Society in 1972 that dieldrin in the fishes' diet upset the delicate balance of amino acids. His experiments showed that dieldrin slowed activity of the liver enzyme, phenylalanine hydroxylase, resulting in increased levels of phenylalanine. Dr. Mehrle said that no tests had yet shown changes in fish brain function, but that other research had indicated changes in the brain chemistry of fish fed with food containing dieldrin. The similarity between PKU symptoms and those seen in fish may imply damage to the brain by dieldrin, but he cautioned that no direct link has yet been established.

There are at least twenty-five inheritable metabolic diseases leading to mental retardation that can be seen during the fetal stage. Such identification is possible through a technique known as amniocentesis. Small amounts of the fluid environment that surrounds the infant as it nestles inside its mother are drawn off, and the cells it contains — from the skin of the fetus or the sac it has been floating in — are studied to determine fetal health or genetic damage. Fetologists, as the specialists concerned with the fetus are called, can get valuable clues from the fetal cells and fluid. Among these are such things as chromosomal abnormalities, fetal age and sex, illnesses due to poisons absorbed from organisms in the system, maternal diabetes, and Rh disease, a blood disorder that can be treated by transfusing fresh blood into the fetus as it lies in the uterus. Now one of the most exciting fields in medicine, fetology may eventually save thousands of babies who abort spontaneously and enable surgeons to operate on malformed and diseased fetuses long before they are born. It may also bring about the very real possibility that scientists will manipulate and rearrange genes to correct birth defects at the time of conception.

Among the conditions that produce severe mental retardation that can be diagnosed through amniocentesis are galactosemia, Tay-Sachs disease, Hurler's syndrome, and Down's syndrome, or Mongolism.

In galactosemia, an enzyme defect prevents the body from using sugar properly. If the condition is untreated (treatment usually involves a milk-free diet to cut off the supply of the milk sugar, galactose), retardation, cataracts, malnutrition, and death can result.

Tay-Sachs disease was first observed in the 1880s by Dr. Warren Tay and Dr. Bernard Sachs. It occurs chiefly among Jewish children, and is usually fatal in the early years of life. An inherited disorder, it is caused by an accumulation of fatty substances in the brain cells, and there is little, if any, treatment. (So-called storage diseases such as Tay-Sachs are usually caused by lack of an enzyme that, under normal circumstances, directs the breakdown of fatty substances or other cell products. In Tay-Sachs disease, the deficient enzyme is known as hexosaminidase A, or hex A for short.) The disorder is marked by loss of coordination because the nervous system deteriorates rapidly, and a child so afflicted becomes unable to grasp objects, loses his sight, and eventually cannot eat or even smile.

In Hurler's syndrome, also called gargoylism, mental deterioration is coupled with a dwarfed stature, grotesque facial features, and an enlargement of the liver and spleen. Accumulated carbohydrates and fats in the brain and liver, the result of a metabolic defect, are a chemical sign of this inherited disorder. Recently, scientists at the

National Institute of Arthritis, Metabolism and Digestive Diseases reported that they had pinpointed the biochemical defect. In cultures of cells from patients with Hurler's syndrome, they found a deficiency of the enzyme iduronidase, which is essential to the normal metabolism of carbohydrates called mucopolysaccharides. (Metabolism, a term used frequently in science, refers to the process by which the body transforms food into the tissue and energy it needs.)

Abnormal chromosomes, those threadlike bits that carry our genes, or the wrong number of chromosomes in the fertilized human egg, may also be responsible for the birth of a defective child. This latter is the case in Down's syndrome, a genetic disorder that occurs in about one out of every 600 births and accounts for some 10 percent of the people in residential facilities for the mentally retarded. Children with the disease have a characteristic set of facial features including slightly slanted eyes, folds of skin in the inner part of each eye, a flattened nose bridge, protruding tongue, square-shaped ears, and little fingers that curve inward. They also are short, with protruding abdomens, have congenital heart disease as well as mental retardation, and are more prone to develop leukemia than normal children. Their I.Q.s range in the 30s and 50s, sometimes as high as the 60s and 70s. First described in 1866 by the English physician Langdon Down, the syndrome is identifiable through amniocentesis. Cells in the fluid are examined under a microscope and the chromosomes are literally counted. The normal fertilized egg contains 46, 23 from the mother and 23 from the father. But in the majority of children with Down's syndrome, there is an extra chromosome — the number 21 chromosome — making a total of 47. The reason for the surplus genetic material is not known.

There is no specific treatment for Mongolism, despite claims that are made from time to time for various combinations of drugs. Some investigators have administered serotonin to children with the disorder, which, according to Dr. Murray Feingold, director of the Center for Genetic Counseling and Birth Defects Evaluation at Tufts–New England Medical Center, results in increased body tone. However, he points out, it is not known what effect it has on the child's intelligence. Dr. Feingold also notes that children with Down's syndrome who are institutionalized have a lower I.Q. than those who stay at home, the reason being that the child reared at home receives greater stimulation and attention. "If the parents have accepted the diagnosis and have given love and attention to the child," he says, "their brothers and sisters will follow suit. Many children with Down's syndrome are the last born in the family, and the older brothers and sisters usually take great joy and satisfaction in looking after their younger sibling. As the normal children grow older and bring friends home, problems may arise. But they are greatly reduced if the years prior to this point have been handled with sound judgment and good common sense." Dr. Feingold adds: "Most children with Down's syndrome are 'too smart' for the state schools while others, more severely retarded children, need the space. Because of the love and attention these children receive at home, they generally do better than the institutionalized child with Down's. Schools should be available to these children in their communities to help them achieve their potential."

Today, genetic counseling is available for prospective parents in many major medical centers. Before the woman plans to conceive, the couple can be screened for genetic flaws and advised about the risk of pregnancy. The woman's age must be taken into consideration, too. For instance, if she is twenty-five years old, she has a chance of one in 2,500 of having a child with Down's syndrome. If she is thirty-five, the risk increases to one in 350; at forty, one in 100; and at age forty-five, one out of 50. Screening for genetic defects is extremely important if there has been a history of such defects or mental retardation in the family. If there has been no screening and a high-risk woman has become pregnant, amniocentesis is performed, and if chromosomal difficulties turn up therapeutic abortion may be considered. (In Tay-Sachs disease, there is a 25 percent risk with each pregnancy of having a child with the disorder if both parents carry the Tay-Sachs gene. There is a 50 percent risk that each child will be a carrier, like his parents, and a 25 percent chance that each will be free of the gene.)

Equally as fascinating as amniocentesis is another new diagnostic technique that is somewhat like the palm-reading one sees at carnivals and amusement parks. Known as dermatoglyphics, which means "skin carvings," it has enabled geneticists to detect a number of conditions — including Mongolism, leukemia, heart disease, and schizophrenia — by close examination of the whorls, ridges, loops, and arches on palm prints.

Fingerprinting is not a new science. The Chinese used such prints in the eighth century to stamp approval on business contracts. In 1901, Sir Edward Richard Henry, commissioner of London's Metropolitan Police, devised the system of fingerprinting and classification generally used today, the official, recognized method of positively identifying human beings. It is extremely doubtful that two people will have the same fingerprints; one estimate is that duplication is not likely to occur in 10,000 years. (Up to now, not a single duplication has been found.) A person's handprint pattern is formed in the first four months before his birth. Mark Twain referred to it as a "natal autograph."

In a recent report in *Medical World News,* Dr. Fred Rosner of Maimonides Medical Center in Brooklyn was quoted as saying that dermatoglyphics can be an absolute diagnosis for Mongolism. "Because there is a combination of features, you can just show me the palms without ever showing me the child, and we can make an absolute and positive diagnosis," he said. The best sign is the so-called simian line on the palm. Seen in a number of disorders, it replaces the two horizontal lines that run partway across most palms. It does, however, take more than a strange line to diagnose Mongolism. Researchers know, for instance, that such children have a marked reduction in finger whorls and an increase in finger loops; signs also occur on the feet.

The fetal period is a most precarious time and, aside from the genetic defects the developing infant can inherit, a number of outside agents also affect him. For example, research has demonstrated that children born to women who smoke ten or more cigarettes a day when pregnant are slower readers and less well adjusted at age seven than children born of nonsmoking mothers. Loud noises, such as the boom of a jet plane breaking the sound barrier, may harm infants at birth, and it has also been suggested that children born to mothers suffering from severe emotional strain during pregnancy cry more and have more stomach ailments than those born to more relaxed mothers.

Drugs can affect the developing fetus in many harmful ways. Infants born to mothers addicted to narcotics like heroin, for instance, often display withdrawal symptoms that may be fatal if not treated quickly. Some medications that have produced cleft palate in the offspring of mice and rats who received them in early pregnancy have been linked to cleft palate or cleft lip in the children of epileptic mothers who took the drugs. In 1971, doctors at Massachusetts General Hospital reported that mothers of seven out of eight young women who developed a rare form of cancer had taken a widely used synthetic hormone during pregnancy — twenty years before. (The hormone is called stilbestrol, and had been given to thousands of women to prevent the likelihood of pregnancy loss in high-risk pregnancies.) The results of the study suggested that it was unwise to administer the hormone to women early in pregnancy. There was the celebrated thalidomide tragedy of 1962 and 1963, when the sedative was responsible for the birth of thousands of deformed babies. More recently, the physician who discovered the devastating effects of thalidomide, Dr. William McBride, charged that another drug, widely prescribed as an antidepressant, may be more potentially dangerous than thalidomide, and that it could cause babies to be born without arms if their mothers took it during early pregnancy. Even aspirin, that popular pain-killer found in virtually every home in the world, has been associated, in high doses, with congenital malformations in the offspring of mothers who took it during pregnancy.

Goodbye to Bedlam

Just as medications can cause physical fetal malformations, so too can they cause mental retardation. While it must be emphasized that most drugs do not automatically bring about fetal deformities, the potential danger is great and extreme caution is required when prescribing for pregnant women or when administering medication to the newborn. The developing brain of the unborn child is utterly dependent on the mother, in whom it nestles, for its nourishing blood-borne oxygen. Any agent, therefore, that lowers blood pressure — such as hypotensive drugs, tranquilizers, and anesthetics — can cause fetal distress with subsequent mental impairment. The anticonvulsants have been linked to mild mental deficiency in the offspring of women who took the drugs for epilepsy while pregnant. Cretinism, a severe thyroid deficiency characterized by mental shortcomings and physical deformity, has been known to result from the administration of radioiodine, a radioactive isotope of iodine used in the treatment of thyroid gland disorders, to women not known to be pregnant. Vitamin K, sulfa drugs, and some antibiotics have been linked to a serious form of jaundice in the newborn that often results in mental retardation. It is known that LSD can damage chromosomes in human blood cells and there have been reports of shattered chromosomes in the babies of mothers who took it while pregnant.

At the 1971 meeting of the Association for Research in Nervous and Mental Disease, Dr. Frances O. Kelsey, director of scientific investigations for the FDA's Bureau of Drugs, noted: "Only about 20 percent of congenital defects are ascribable to genetic factors or known environmental hazards, including drugs and infectious diseases.

The question remains as to what role drug therapy may play in the remaining 80 percent. Surveys conducted even after the thalidomide episode indicate on the average between three and four drugs are prescribed during pregnancy."

Diseases caused by viruses and germs can also result in mental retardation. Rubella, or German measles, is one of these. Less contagious than ordinary measles and frequent in young adults, the virus-caused disease is not particularly serious unless it afflicts a woman during her first three months of pregnancy. When this occurs, the baby may be born with a mental deficiency, heart disease, cataracts, and hearing difficulties. Fortunately, a protective vaccine has been developed that can be given to women prior to pregnancy. Syphilis in pregnant women is responsible for a number of neurological problems and mental retardation in the offspring, as is the infecting agent that causes a severe central nervous system disease called toxoplasmosis. Researchers are also studying the possible effects on the fetus of such disorders as mumps, hepatitis, flu, pneumonia, and cold viruses.

Brain damage resulting from complications during delivery of the baby, X rays taken during pregnancy, postnatal infections, physical abuse by beating on the head (the so-called battered child syndrome), lead poisoning (common in slum areas where children innocently chew bits of lead-based paint that has peeled from old walls and windowsills), and various convulsive disorders and infantile spasms — all of these may be responsible for some degree of mental deficiency. There also seems to be a link between epilepsy and retardation. One estimate is that nearly 25 percent of those in institutions suffer also from epilepsy, and that around 90 percent of youngsters afflicted by serious spasms or seizures in infancy become mentally retarded. These seizures are not to be confused with the convulsions that can accompany certain feverish disorders and that are generally harmless.

A good bit of attention is being paid today to dietary deficiencies — malnutrition and lack of nutrition — and the part they play in mental deterioration and learning. There is mounting evidence, in fact, that malnutrition, particularly protein deficiency during the early stages of life — in the womb and within a year after birth — may be tied to permanent mental retardation as well as to poor physical growth. In PKU, it was noted, an amino acid found in most protein foods is not used up by the infant but, instead, builds up in the blood and damages the brain. A special diet that eliminates certain foods can correct the situation.

More than fifty years ago, experiments with rats demonstrated that nutritional inadequacies had an adverse effect on the central nervous system. Current studies not only have confirmed this but have shown that learning and behavior also are affected, that the retardation caused may often be permanent and irreversible no matter how adequate the later diet, and that lagging brain development may carry over into another generation or more.

While the baby is in the womb, his brain (nearly half of whose gray matter is protein) begins to grow rapidly, and by the time he is three years old, 80 percent of his adult brain weight has been achieved. At the same time, his body has accomplished only 20 percent of its ultimate growth. (In rats, 80 percent of brain growth occurs by the time the animals are a month old.) Because of this speedy growth during the early years, the brain is quite susceptible to the effects of malnutrition. And the key appears to be protein malnutrition. In the womb, the baby gets the vital amino acids his brain cells need from the protein his mother eats. After birth, the infant is supplied with aminos from his mother's milk and from other foods. When the flow of aminos is reduced, while the mother is carrying her child or after birth, brain growth is stunted and learning is slowed.

Scientists have been able to prove this in a variety of experiments. They have shown, for example, that depriving pregnant rats of protein results in fewer nerve cells in the offspring's brains. They have also shown that the levels of some enzymes and amino acids in their brains are altered when they are fed diets low in protein. In one study, groups of rats — 1, 6, and 12 months old — were fed low-protein diets for four to six months. Visual perception and learning ability were impaired in each of the age groups, but the effects were more noticeable in the month-old animals. At Cornell University, a group reported that pigs fed a low-protein diet for two months after weaning grew up as slow learners and were easily upset. It was also found that general food restriction, with its resulting lack of nutrition, did not have a significant effect on the animals' ability to solve experimental problems, though it did cause behavioral changes. When protein was withheld, however, not only were the behavioral changes associated with general food restriction present, but the animals' ability to do well on learning tests also was affected.

While laboratory mice have been called miniature humans, they are not, of course, and one must be cautious when applying the results of animal research to human beings. To perform similar experiments on humans is morally unacceptable; few researchers would want, or be allowed, to deliberately withhold nourishing protein from infants. Thus animal studies are vitally important and do tell us something, particularly when laboratory results are compared with field observations of humans who live in a poor environment, say, in an underdeveloped country, and whose eating habits leave much to be desired. At an international conference on malnutrition, learning, and behavior held at the Massachusetts Institute of Technology in 1967, Dr. Paul B. Pearson, president of the Nutrition Foundation, warned that the results of animal studies cannot be extrapolated to man. But, he added, "The fact that pre- and post-natal malnutrition of rats and pigs adversely affects learning and behavioral patterns is consistent with field observations on humans. It is generally felt that adults who have had second degree malnutrition during early childhood usually show a lower level of intellectual performance than people reared in a similar environment but with an adequate diet. Children suffering from malnutrition show psychological changes in behavioral patterns, mental apathy and loss of drive and incentive."

One of the few scientists who has been able to study the effects of malnutrition in human populations is Dr. Joaquin Cravioto, a Mexico City pediatrician. Dr. Cravioto has had a good deal of experience caring for children suffering from a protein-deficiency disease called kwashiorkor. First discovered in 1933, this disease is found in a number of tropical and subtropical countries.

It occurs primarily in infants who have been weaned onto starchy food, such as manioc root in Africa, that contains very little protein. The child gets plenty of calories and appears to be well nourished, to the point of developing a characteristic "pot belly" and generalized swelling of body tissues. He is actually suffering from serious malnutrition because of the protein deficiency and its accompanying lack of essential amino acids.

Dr. Cravioto and his associates studied infants with kwashiorkor in Mexico and Guatemala, and were able to show that the short stature for the age of the children — the height retardation was due to malnutrition in the early years — was accompanied by poorer performance on psychological tests. As kwashiorkor patients became better nourished, their behavioral skills improved somewhat, but there was an interesting exeption. Infants who underwent nutritional rehabilitation before they were six months old continued to be deficient in their test behavior, suggesting that acute malnourishment during those first six months could be permanently damaging to I.Q. and behavior. In another study, scientists examined the brains of infants who had died of marasmus, a form of undernutrition marked by gross weight loss and a wasting of fat and muscle, and found they had undergone abnormal changes similar to those found in the brains of young starved animals. In still another survey, a group of South African children who had been severely malnourished in infancy were watched carefully for more than eleven years. Though the children seemed to have recovered physically, there were noticeable differences in I.Q. (more than 20 points) between them and a group of average children. Also, the heads of the once malnourished children never reached normal size, and the children had continuing visual and motor abnormalities.

"It is apparent that many questions, particularly those related to a causal relationship between nutrient deficiency and mental development, remain to be answered," Dr. Cravioto told the MIT conference. "But it is clear that the available knowledge leaves no doubts about the strong association between the antecedent of severe malnutrition in infancy and the sub-optimal performance at the school age. It is also obvious . . . that the consequences of early malnutrition will be greatest when after rehabilitation the child continues to live in an environment in which both social and nutritional circumstances will continue to be poor and noxious for his growth and development."

(In 1972, two MIT scientists discovered that each meal eaten by experimental rats quickly changed the animals' brain levels of serotonin. The finding was considered rather surprising in light of the common belief that the brain is affected nutritionally only by long-term malnutrition. In their experiment, Dr. Richard J. Wurtman and Dr. John Fernstrom fed special meals to the rats and saw that food rich in carbohydrates increased the serotonin level in the brain. The meals containing 40 percent protein depressed the serotonin levels; meals of 24 percent protein did not change the amount of serotonin. Reporting in *Science*, the researchers said that the amount of serotonin in the brain may provide it with important information about a broad range of metabolic states. "It is still too early in our research to know for sure," Dr. Wurtman said, "but serotonin may, for example, tell the animal to curl up and go to sleep after a meal or, conversely, to search for more food." They said they planned to begin looking for other chemical substances in the rat's brain that might respond rapidly to changes in diet. Dr. Wurtman added: "We also expect the same kind of rapid changes in people, and will be developing methods to determine how the human brain responds to each meal a person eats. Our results could have implications for physicians who prescribe psychotherapeutic drugs, many of which seem to work by affecting the release or actions of brain serotonin. In order to obtain optimal therapeutic results, physicians may have to give more consideration to their patients' diets.")

While it may be too late to help those who were malnourished during infancy (although scientists are seeking a chemical way to right nutrition-damaged brains), it is not too late to help those yet unborn. In the United States alone an estimated 20 million people suffer from malnutrition. This semistarvation exists, for the most part, in urban and rural low-income areas, and the reason for it was stated by President Nixon at the 1969 White House Conference on Nutrition. "Millions of Americans are simply too poor to feed their families properly," the president said. In the fourth annual report of the President's Committee on Mental Retardation it was noted that upward of 25 million Americans live on incomes of less than $3,300 a year for a family of four, and that half of them, including some five million children, live in households having an annual income of $2,200 or less. To maintain an adequate diet, such families would have to spend over half of their income for food, and almost no one can realistically budget so large a part of income for eating. Several programs and approaches have been tried to help those who have been economically and nutritionally shortchanged to share in this country's prosperity. It is possible to eradicate hunger in our land of plenty, and with it a cause of mental retardation.

But if the disorder is to be prevented — and it can be in about half the cases through adequate nutrition, early diagnosis as in PKU, prevention of diseases like rubella, and through loving attention and a stable environment — the support of an enlightened and educated public is necessary. And health professionals should not be excluded from such education. In the Boston University study cited earlier, it was revealed that while many of the nurses surveyed experienced compassion and understanding for the retarded, several pediatric nurses admitted a feeling of repulsion at the thought of having to care for such a child. Physicians, particularly the doctor in private practice who sees children in their first years of life, the time when the chances of reversing the disorder are best, have an important role to play in the early identification and treatment of mental retardation. This is particularly true in what is termed sociocultural retardation. In such cases, according to a 1965 report from the American Medical Association's Conference on Mental Retardation, enrichment of the child's environment begun early enough may save the child from a lifetime handicap.

As in Mongolism, the trend today is away from institutionalization of a retarded child. A five-year study by a Boston University psychologist, Dr. Frances K. Grossman, found, in fact, that growing up with a retarded brother or sister in the house can be a positive experience that develops an unusual degree of understanding in normal children. In a book published in 1972, Dr. Grossman focused not on the retarded child but on his siblings; she found that these children benefited by having a greater understanding of people, more tolerance of human frailty, more compassion, more sensitivity to prejudice and its consequences, and more appreciation of their own good health and intelligence. Other positive effects were a sense of family closeness and a pride in the family's ability to cope as a unit. In families not suffering from major financial hardships, Dr. Grossman reported, the more the retarded child was at home growing up with other children the better his brothers and sisters dealt with the situation, the more they liked the slower child, and the more they saw him as a human being with feelings, as a person. Where the presence of a retarded child had an adverse effect, she found, it often was because society stood in the way and fed the belief that retardation is inevitably tragic and traumatic for everyone in the family. Normal children affected adversely by the retarded siblings experienced such feelings as shame and guilt. Some felt somehow tainted or defective themselves; others felt guilty for being in good health and for harboring negative feelings about the retarded child. Some felt they were neglected by their parents, who were preoccupied with the deficient child.

As an example of the positive effects that can be gained, Dr. Grossman mentioned one child, James, the second oldest of eight children, the youngest of whom, six-year-old Marty, had Down's syndrome.

"Marty is the person in my family I like the most," James said. "We consider him heaven-sent. He teaches us so much. He is innocent all the time. When you are grown up you tend to become sophisticated and see things from a complicated point of view. And then when you come to Marty — you see how he does it — it sort of brings you down to where you should be. It makes me appreciative of how much I really have when I see how limited he is. And I never thought of myself as being very smart, but compared to him I realize I have a lot of unused potential, where it seems he is using everything he's got."

More than 95 percent of the five million retarded live in the community, and 85 percent of those afflicted are capable of working. The retarded, in fact, have been described as the greatest untapped source of manpower in the labor market because it is the mildly retarded who make up the vast bulk of the retarded population. And yet ignorance still prevails. There are still those in our midst who shun the retarded, continue to deprive them, and who do not yet realize that these children can benefit from an education, that in fact they have a right to education under our Constitution's equal protection clause.

Something can be done about mental retardation. But not until poverty is brought under control, not until educational and recreational programs for the retarded are expanded, not until the old myths are dead.

6 Psychosomatic Disorders

In discussing neuroses, it was noted that in hysteria emotional conflict is transformed into physical symptoms such as paralysis and numbness. The term "psychosomatic" (from the Greek words *psyche*, for mind, and *soma*, for body) is used in a broader sense when referring to physical illnesses that result from psychological disturbances.

Just about everyone has experienced a queasy stomach on the first day of school or suffered a splitting headache after some tense situation. And few, if any of us, have not known what it means to be "worried sick." These reactions are garden-variety forms of physical upset that can be brought on by our emotions, and they are usually self-limiting or, in the case of a mild headache, dispelled by an aspirin. Emotional conflict, however, which occurs when the mental turmoil is drawn out and unresolved, can express itself in physical ways that are far more serious, even painful, than the ordinary stomach upset. In instances like this, the sufferer's physical problem not only needs to be treated as though it were caused by a virus or accident, but the patient must be treated psychologically as well.

There are many such conditions, among which can be asthma, ulcers, hay fever, migraine headache, colitis, arthritis, palpitations of the heart, hypertension, skin rashes, backache, and an overactive thyroid. It has even been suggested recently that cancer is associated with psychological factors.

The disorders that are linked to emotions are as real as those caused by the physical agents that are known to cause disease. It is not easy, however, to sift out how much of any given physical ailment is due to the psyche and how much to the soma itself. For example, a disease-causing virus may be lying dormant in a person's body for some time and be activated by depression or tension. The mind does exert power over the body, and vice versa; there is interaction between them. In the chapters on schizophrenia and mental retardation, we have seen that organic causes can be at the heart of abnormal behavior. In psychosomatic illness, the reverse is true: the way the mind behaves affects bodily function. How this occurs has much to do with the nervous system and the endocrine glands, both of which direct organ function. Chemicals, physiology, and emotions combine to bring on mind-originated ills. Just as defects in the body's chemistry can cause mental retardation and may be linked to schizophrenia, so, too, can chemical reactions trigger the ailments mentioned earlier. To understand the process, a brief review of the pertinent physiology might be helpful.

The nervous system is an extremely delicate and complicated network that sends its branches into every part of the human body. In control of this vast system is the brain, a three-pound lump of wrinkled gray matter whose rather unattractive form and spongy composition give little indication that it is a master computer infinitely more elaborate and capable than any of the electronic brains it has invented. From its vantage point atop the body, the brain oversees a communications system made up of billions of nerve cells (neurons), each with a special job, tiny connecting nerve branches, and the spinal cord over which electrochemical messages are transmitted and received. The brain's neurons and those in other parts of the body have electrical charges created by chemical action. Each person has his own distinctive brain wave pattern, the result of electrical current charge. This electrical activity may be traced by a technique known as electroencephalography, by which tiny wires (electrodes) are attached to the scalp and connected to a vacuum tube amplifier. There, they are magnified some one million times and made to activate an electromagnetic pen that writes the electroencephalogram, or EEG, on a moving strip of paper. The EEG is used to determine the death of an individual: when the brain wave expresses itself as a flat line for a certain length of time, the brain cells are considered to be dead.

The brain is synonymous with the mind, with intelligence, memory, judgment, learning, and creativity. Every time we hate, love, fear, and crave it is at work, controlling our dreams, our fantasies, our real behavior. Since it is connected by nerves to all parts of the body from head to toe, the brain is also in charge of other actions. Every time we move, feel, hear, smell, speak, see, write, feel pain, and breathe, electrochemical messages are pulsing back and forth from the brain to the far reaches of the body. These bursts of activity when neurons "fire" go on every moment of our lives, when we are asleep as well as awake. If, for example, we step on a tack barefoot, pain nerves are activated. The neurons are stimulated, and they beam an electrical pulse-message to the brain, warning it of unpleasantness. Instantly, the brain sends a message to the foot muscles, ordering them to pull the foot away from the tack.

The nervous system is divided into two main parts, central and autonomic; the latter is subdivided into two other systems, sympathetic and parasympathetic, which delicately balance each other to keep the body on a healthy, steady course. The central nervous system, made up of the brain and the spinal cord, supervises all our voluntary activities — our muscular movements, consciousness, and mental activity. The autonomic nervous system, linked by nerves to the central nervous system, takes care of our involuntary actions — those things our bodies must do, such as heart and lung action, the digestive process, operation of the glands and function of the smooth muscle tissue of hollow organs, to name but a few. This control by the autonomic system is exerted over nerves that feed from both the parasympathetic and sympathetic divisions directly into the body's internal organs, among them the heart, intestine, stomach, liver, pancreas, bladder, reproductive organs, kidneys, and salivary glands. The sympathetic nervous system may be likened to the accelerator of an automobile, particularly in an emergency situation. In times of stress, for instance, it reacts by "stepping on the gas" to flood the bloodstream with adrenaline, a hormone manufactured by the endocrine glands that constricts the blood vessels and drives blood pressure up. The heart beats faster, the pupils of the eyes expand, or dilate, the muscles tense; gastric juices and intestinal peristalsis (involuntary muscle movement that propels food along) are inhibited, thus impairing digestion. The parasympathetic system strives to restore the balance that has been upset by the sympathetic's somewhat heavy-handed response, which it does after the storm of stress has subsided. Under its direction the heartbeat is slowed, blood pressure drops, the pupils constrict, and the secretions of most glands are stimulated. The flow of gastric juices is stepped up and peristalsis and digestive activity are stimulated.

It is easy to understand, in view of this meshing of the nervous and endocrine systems and their connection to the bodily organs, how stress and emotions alter the body's vital functions to produce psychosomatic disorders.

One of the most common stress-induced physical ailments is peptic ulcer, a disease of the gastrointestinal tract. An ulcer is an open sore in the lining of the stomach or in the duodenum, the beginning of the small intestine. Ulcers usually result when gastric secretions, mainly hydrochloric acid, irritate and actually digest the mucous membrane that lines the stomach's walls. When we have food in our stomach, gastric juices are stimulated to aid in digestion. We also secrete acid when we see or smell food, a reflex action much like when our mouths water in anticipation of a tempting meal. Emotions can also step up the flow of gastric juices, and some people secrete more acid than others. The autonomic nervous system and the endocrine glands, as noted, can trigger acid production in the stomach when a person is upset and thus create an ulcer. Not everyone who secretes acid, of course, gets an ulcer, and why this is so is not totally understood. Some people may have a predisposition to the disorder, and others simply may secrete more acid.

Researchers are still trying to determine just what combination (if it is a combination) of psychological and biological factors results in diseases such as ulcers (and, as indicated earlier, schizophrenia). What is important in the case of ulcers (and in any psychosomatic disease) is that while the disorder may be treated medically or with a surgical procedure — such as cutting the vagus nerve, the nerve running from the brain to the stomach, to block acid-producing impulses — unless the patient is treated for his emotional stress his ulcer probably will not heal easily. Too often, sufferers refuse to accept that their emotions are at fault and simply demand that physicians cure them. They do not ask that the doctors *help* them.

Ulcerative colitis is another illness that may be linked to emotions, although physicians disagree on this. The disease, which frequently strikes young adults, is marked by attacks of bloody diarrhea and sometimes necessitates surgical removal of the lower bowel. Overstimulation of the parasympathetic system, which produces spasms of the colon (the large intestine), has been connected to the disorder by some researchers. Investigators have also discovered that an enzyme that rises during anxious moments is found in higher concentrations in some patients with the disease. Other studies have shown that bouts of ulcerative colitis may occur a day or two after some emotional upheaval.

Asthma and hay fever, both allergic diseases ordinarily associated with sensitivity to a host of substances, are two other mind-body illnesses within the autonomic nervous system. The most serious of the common allergic diseases, asthma, results when the involuntary muscles of the smaller bronchial passages go into spasm. Endocrine changes, such as in puberty, pregnancy and menstruation, are known to influence the frequency and severity of asthmatic attacks, and it has been shown that how the susceptible person reacts to the irritating substances, or allergens, sometimes depends on his emotional state. Mere exposure, then, to allergens such as house dust and pollens would not necessarily mean that an attack is inevitable. Investigators have also found that frequently asthmatic patients are insecure, lack confidence, and have had closer than ordinary relationships with their mothers. A few years ago, it was discovered that there had been a sharp rise in asthma among Puerto Ricans and blacks in New York City, and psychosomatic specialists expressed the opinion that the increase was partially due to tensions created by the fight for equality under the civil rights movement.

We have already seen how high blood pressure (known medically as hypertension, a disorder that afflicts 23 million Americans and kills more than 60,000 of them a year) can be caused by stimulation of the sympathetic nervous system during stress periods. Suppressed rage and hostility are chief among these stresses that may be responsible for chronic hypertension if not released either in a physical way or through some sort of self-assertive behavior. For example, the individual who wants very much to make a firm decision but lacks the courage to do so is regarded as a good candidate for high blood pressure. One psychiatrist has likened this situation to stepping on the accelerator with the emergency brake on. People with high blood pressure also seem to be prone to ulcers and migraine headaches.

Goodbye to Bedlam

In a recent set of behavioral laboratory experiments conducted by Harvard investigators at Boston City Hospital, five out of seven patients were actually able to reduce their systolic blood pressure by 9 percent through their conscious reaction to external stimuli such as tones, lights, and projected slides. (Systolic pressure is that exerted on the wall of an artery during contraction of the heart muscle.) The patients were told that they would be paid $5 a session to come to the laboratory and have their blood pressure measured automatically for approximately an hour while they sat quietly. They were also told that no medications would be used, but that the procedures might help in lowering their blood pressure. During the sessions, each patient sat in an isolation chamber that contained a screen onto which slides were projected. A small microphone was fixed under the blood pressure cuff that picked up what are called Korotkoff sounds, which are produced by the blood flow through the brachial artery when the cuff pressure is applied. A relatively low systolic blood pressure, indicated by absence of the Korotkoff sound, was fed back to the patients on each heartbeat. This was indicated simultaneously by a brief flash of light and a tone of moderate intensity. The patients were told that the tone and the light were desirable, and that they should try to make them appear. As a reward, after each twenty presentations of tone and light, a photographic slide equivalent to five cents was shown for five seconds. The slides consisted of scenic pictures and reminders of the amount of money earned. When the experiment was over, the doctors were able to determine that there had been a noticeable drop in the average blood pressure.

"Elevated arterial blood pressure increases the risk of coronary artery disease and cerebrovascular accidents," commented Dr. Herbert Benson, who was in charge of the experiment. "This increased risk is lessened by lowering blood pressure. At the present time the means of doing this are largely pharmacological. In our experiments, systolic blood pressure could be decreased by operant conditioning techniques (behavior training) in five out of seven patients with essential hypertension."

Such experiments tie in with what has come to be known as biofeedback training, whereby the mind is used to control the involuntary nervous system. Biofeedback harnesses the body's natural rhythms — brain waves and the autonomic functions mentioned earlier — to electronic monitors that enable an individual to "see" his heartbeat inked out on a graph or "hear" his brain waves in the form of a series of high-pitched beeps. By "watching" such usually unconscious occurrences like blood pressure and heart and lung action and listening to different kinds of brainwaves, a person might be able to influence his physical and mental well-being. Unfortunately, biofeedback has become quite popular with do-it-yourself, amateur psychologists, who can obtain relatively inexpensive biofeedback devices now being sold to the general public.

In the case of brain waves there are a number of different wave lengths, classified as alpha, beta, theta, and delta, and each is associated with some mental state. It has been known for some time that during periods of deep meditation and relaxation, Zen and yoga devotees generate alpha waves almost exclusively. Beta waves appear to be emitted during anxious moments, delta during sleep, and theta in periods of creativity. By listening to these waves, amplified electronically, one is often able to regulate his mental state and, some scientists believe, relax without the use of medication, improve memory and the power of concentration, and sleep better.

Some two hundred scientists are now believed to be testing biofeedback techniques, and while there is some skepticism, researchers have demonstrated that it should continue to be explored because its medical potential could indeed be boundless.

High blood pressure, again, has a good deal to do with such disorders as stroke and a range of cardiac complications. Recently, some physicians from the University of Rochester School of Medicine reported that abrupt changes in mood from depression to an emotional high of anger or elation and then back again may touch off a sudden fatal heart attack in persons with a history of heart disease. In the study, which involved twenty-six men who died suddenly, the doctors noted a pattern of events that led to death: the man would be a high-risk patient because of heart disease history, he had been depressed for a week or several months before death, and he had strong feelings of anger, anxiety, or even elation just before he died. The doctors also found that sudden death from a heart attack, or abnormal heart rhythms, occurred within twenty-four hours of the first noteworthy symptoms. The doctors, who reported their findings in the *Archives of Internal Medicine,* suggested that death probably occurred when the patient reverted to his usual depressed condition after being highly emotionally aroused. The accompanying drop in pulse rate and blood pressure caused the fatal heart attack. In other words, the contrast between the slowed down "blues" state and the

stress the patient experienced just before death was over-
whelming, and the patients, already weakened by heart
disease, could not handle it.

Migraine headaches, the cause of which is generally
unknown, have been linked to tension, fatigue, depression,
and irritability. They are also often found in association
with other psychosomatic disorders such as asthma,
hypertension, and hives, an itchy skin rash. The latter,
which may also have an allergic origin, may be brought
on by emotional upset, and doctors have found that controlling stressful situations often brings relief. Skin disorders are associated with emotions through the autonomic
nervous system, which controls the skin's blood vessels.
These vessels react to shifts in emotions, causing skin
eruptions and also the phenomenon we know as blushing.

Blushing, which occurs only in humans and usually on
the face, may be related to shame, modesty, or confusion.
One recent report from the University of Rochester suggested that a blusher is unconsciously trying to tell others
that what they might be thinking of him at a specific
moment is false. If, for instance, someone blushes when
hearing an off-color joke, he is saying, "You might think I
am an immoral person because I have been listening to
this story and said nothing. I don't want you to think I am
that kind of person, and I don't want to appear that way,
so I will prove that I am not by blushing." The same may
be true when a person trips and falls in public. He may be
telling anyone nearby, "Maybe you think I'm clumsy
because I've done this stupid thing, but I don't want to
seem that way so I am blushing to tell you I am not."

Some researchers believe that arthritis, the great crippler disease involving the body's joints and other connec-
tive tissues, may be psychosomatic. Emotional stress may

touch off an attack, but exactly how this might happen is not clearly understood. There has been speculation that patients with the disease repress hostility that bursts out in the skeletal muscles. One investigator found that when he administered norepinephrine, an adrenal hormone, to dogs, they developed symptoms strikingly like those of arthritis. It remains to be seen, however, whether drugs that block adrenal response will benefit arthritics.

One of the more fascinating theories about emotional linkup to disease deals with cancer. While the evidence is far from conclusive, some researchers have put forth the tantalizing suggestion that there is such a phenomenon as the "cancer personality." In 1971, at an American Cancer Society seminar, two psychologists discussed such a personality, concluding that it would represent an uptight, defensive, Middle American member of the Establishment, conformist and correct in behavior. The same assessment, the researchers said, seems to hold true for the patient who suffers from rheumatoid arthritis. "Cancer patients are the Protestant ethic, the nice guys who are committed to doing what the next guy does, appearing correctly and being a kind person," said Dr. Claus Bahnson of the Pennsylvania Department of Mental Health. He added that if he were to allow himself a prediction, he would say that if a person had all of the characteristics he described he would have a 30 percent chance of being a cancer patient. "If he had some of them, it would be about a 10 percent chance," the doctor said, cautioning that his estimate was off the cuff. Dr. Bahnson had carried out a number of studies that focused on the personalities and life histories of cancer patients. What emerged was the profile of a person who was repressed, who denied feelings that were not socially acceptable, and who was "authoritarian, committed to social norms and who had great difficulty dealing with and expressing anger." Cancer patients also, it was found, repressed all unpleasant states — anxiety, depression, hostility, or guilt — and described their childhood experiences as bleak and dissatisfying. They perceived their mothers as unloving, unprotecting, and unrewarding and their fathers as unprotective and nondemanding.

The other psychologist, Dr. George F. Solomon of Stanford University, said he found similar characteristics in persons prone to rheumatoid arthritis. "People who are repressed, who act pleasant and who deny expressions of hostility seem more prone to the disease," he declared. The basis for the two behavioral scientists' assumptions was the relationship of hormones, which control various bodily functions, to stress, and the relationship between stress states and changes in the body's so-called immune behavior, the mechanism by which infection is warded off. (Rheumatoid arthritis, as was noted in the chapter on schizophrenia, has been associated with a relative deficiency in the immune response.) "Particularly in the area of rodent studies of immune reactions to cancer induced by viruses and other carcinogens," Dr. Bahnson said, "has it become clear that early rearing variables and a number of life stress situations are related to the immune competence of the animal. Russian and American researchers have also noted that manipulations involving the nervous system influence the malignant development in experimental animals. Endocrinological researchers have demonstrated that particular endocrine profiles are associated with the development of cancer in general. Thus, hard-nosed data corroborate the notion that psychological events, mediated by the nervous system, may influence endocrine and immune reactions related to malignancies."

There is some evidence that women who have been recently widowed stand a better chance of developing cancer than other women of the same age. On the other hand, mental hospitals in Great Britain and the Soviet Union, among other countries, have been finding that psychiatric patients seem to have a high level of resistance to cancer. Apparently schizophrenics, more than others, do not die from the disease as frequently as normal individuals, nor do they seem to be stricken with it as often. The discovery has led researchers to suggest that there may be some as yet unidentified immunity factor present in such mental patients.

Says Dr. Thomas P. Hackett, a psychiatrist at the Massachusetts General Hospital, "It is certainly true that many physicians have come to agree that there is a very definite relationship between emotional factors and the onset of the actual disease. We know through some studies done in New York, for example, that the common head cold is found far more frequently in individuals who have had a recent upset. It may be a failed exam or a broken engagement, but there is usually something that upsets the individual's emotional economy just before the infection starts."

Dr. Hackett and another MGH psychiatrist, Dr. Avery D. Weisman, have also described examples of what they refer to as "medical hexes." In one instance, according to a recent report in the *MGH News*, a man in his mid-forties was X-rayed at a West Coast hospital in order to determine the cause of his cough. The X ray confirmed lung cancer. As the months passed, the man lost weight and his cough got worse. He developed the kind of pain that comes with spreading malignancy and he prepared himself psychologically to die. But then another doctor stepped in and suggested a more complete set of X rays. They showed no cancer or, for that matter, any serious illness. The man cheered up, lost the pain, and regained his weight. "It probably isn't fair to call it a hex," said Dr. Hackett, "instead of a misdiagnosis, but in fact that is what it was. The victim of voodoo firmly believes that when a witch doctor singles him out and, as in the case of Australian aborigines, points a bone at him, death will soon follow. A grave is dug for him, and the people, even his closest relatives, treat him as though he were dead. And he does die."

Another version of the "medical hex" is what the MGH psychiatrists call the "anniversary reaction." This occurs in a person who has lost a close relative from coronary disease at a comparatively young age. "When the survivor reaches about the same age, he begins to worry about being struck down by a myocardial infarction [heart attack] and not infrequently he, too, will have a heart attack," says Dr. Hackett. Whether the cause is hereditary, psychological, or both no one knows.

While psychosomatic illnesses are an accepted fact — some say that three out of four cases of illnesses originate in the mind, others that a third of the problems of an acute stage of illness as well as half the problems arising from convalescing start there — it would be a grave mistake to believe that every illness has an emotional basis. To do so would be to overlook the physical cause of disease in many cases, and thus bring disaster on the patient.

In Chapter 8, one way that true psychosomatic illness may be alleviated through group therapy will be discussed.

7 Brain Dysfunction

It has been suggested that damage to the brain has much to do with aberrant behavior. The damage, as we have noted, may be due to chemical problems, lack of adequate blood supply, metal poisoning, birth defects, and the effects of senility.

Today, much attention is being devoted to violent behavior and to the idea that abnormalities of the brain — diseases, or what some have called "electrical storms" — are responsible for crimes of violence. There is no doubt that violence and violent death are everywhere. America's homicide rate is considerably higher than that of other civilized countries. And, contrary to popular opinion, few of the murders we hear about, except those that fall into the gangland category, are coolly planned and executed. Generally, murders are angry, spur-of-the-moment acts committed by ordinary, law-abiding citizens, the "boy next door," "average" and "normal" people who strike out in moments of blind fury, motivated by anger, fear, jealousy, panic, or some other impulse. Everyone, in fact, hides violent impulses. Fortunately, control mechanisms fashioned by both heredity and environment stop most of us before it's too late. Why, then, do people commit violence? Are rioters, sociopaths, and delinquents all suffering from brain disorders?

Many scientists believe that such things as slum conditions and childhood trauma, while they do contribute to violent behavior, do not adequately explain it. They cite ghetto rioting, noting that small numbers of those who live there have participated, and of those still fewer have engaged in murderous assaults. They argue that if slum conditions alone were the cause of violence, then most of the inhabitants of such neighborhoods would be unable to restrain themselves, and such is not the case. A few years ago, some researchers in Boston suggested that the obvious things that go on in an underprivileged neighborhood may have clouded over other possible factors in the rioters who fired on people on the street from snipers' perches and physically assaulted them. They also referred to French and South African studies that indicated that abnormal brain waves occurred six to nine times more frequently in persons found guilty of murder than in the general population. (One English study found that only 1 out of 11 persons convicted of killing in self-defense had abnormal brain-wave patterns, but that they were detected in 11 out of 15 people who killed without apparent motive.)

Studies linking brain derangement, or brain dysfunction, to violent behavior focus on the brain because, as was explained in the previous chapter, it is the single bodily organ vital to behavior, be it violent or peaceful. The brain is strongly influenced by our environment, by what other people say and do. And, as we have seen, it is also an electrical instrument with a distinctive wave pattern that results from electrical current discharge. When the electricity in effect misfires, abnormal behavior may result.

Certain parts of the brain control most activities — such as memory for speech and music, bodily movements, coordination, and balance — that are necessary for us to function as living organisms. The brain is divided into two equal halves, each of those split into five lobes, or sections. We know that damage to these portions of the brain often interferes with normal functioning. Injury to the occipital lobe, for example, can cause blindness. Damage to the frontal lobe may result in personality changes.

Erratic patterns of electrical brain waves, "electrical storms" if you will, already have been associated with certain physical conditions such as epilepsy. These "storms" often occur in the center of the brain's temporal lobe, the chief site of impulse control, when the patient suffers from some epilepsies. They frequently present themselves without outward signs, but they are marked by strange behavior and outbursts of violence. Deeper in the brain is the limbus area, believed to be the site of man's brain early in evolution, a primitive system allied to emotions and one that controls and directs different types of behavior. Some of the "electrical storms" that lead to violence may originate in the limbus. To demonstrate the part these turbulences play in violent behavior, Dr. Frank Ervin and Dr. Vernon Mark of the Massachusetts General Hospital implanted electrodes in the brains of laboratory animals. By stimulating its brains with electrical radio-waves, a cat, for example, could be made to attack anything in its way. Similar reactions have been produced in humans. The doctors have also used electrical stimulation of the brain to treat patients whose epilepsy forces them to erupt in violent rage.

Other experimental studies have produced some equally dramatic results. Neuropsychologists at Purdue University have brought about striking and measurable changes in the behavior of cats and monkeys by manipulating the chemical climate of their brains. Sated animals were made to eat ravenously, and fits of rage were induced. At Tulane, Dr. Robert G. Heath, whose work with schizophrenia was discussed earlier, has planted more than a hundred electrodes at a time into the brains of patients suffering from a wide variety of mental problems and pains. By electrically stimulating the septal region, he has been able to bring on feelings of pleasure and to obliterate the pain. Dr. Heath also feels that by controlling pleasure, one can alter unhealthy patterns of learned behavior and he has reported success in changing the repellent feelings homosexuals feel toward the opposite sex into pleasurable ones.

Some of the pioneering in the field of electrical stimulation of the brain has been done by Dr. Jose M. R. Delgado, professor of physiology at Yale. In 1954, Dr. Delgado demonstrated that he could control psychological phenomena in individual cats, rats, and monkeys. He was able to evoke or inhibit learning, conditioning, response, pain, and pleasure. By stimulating the brain electrically in experiments with humans, he soothed violent patients and relieved pain, and influenced mental functions such as the thinking process, speech, and memory. His most sensational attempt to control aggressive animal behavior came in a bull ring. Standing directly in the path of a charging bull that had electrodes implanted in its brain, he stopped the animal dead in its tracks by radio. In 1970, he and his team were able to establish, for the first time, direct two-way radio communication between an animal's brain (that of a chimpanzee) and a computer. Dr. Delgado also found that in man, the manner in which violence is expressed may depend on the social setting. In one instance, a patient who seemed to be out of control after electrical stimulation refused to attack her doctor. This showed the scientists that she was aware of, and respected, the doctor's rank.

The body's chemistry, of course, may also be a clue to aggressive behavior, just as it is in schizophrenia and mental retardation. The male hormone, for instance, can increase aggressive feelings in adolescents who have feelings of inferiority. A number of drugs can elevate a person's mood, while others can cause depression. These swings seem to be associated with key brain chemicals, and scientists believe that drugs that affect man's emotional state may have an effect on these chemicals, the biogenic amines. How this happens is not quite clear. But it *is* known that the mood-elevating drugs tend to speed up the activity of some of these amines, while the mood-depressing drugs slow them down. This would indicate that the amines have something to do with mood and emotional states. It is still too early to tell whether the amines are involved in violent behavior or in mental disorders that can cause such behavior.

At Princeton, scientists used a drug called carbachol, which imitates the action of a brain chemical believed to be related to the transmission of nerve impulses, to produce some interesting reactions. Twelve rats that normally never killed mice were injected with the drug in the brain area responsible for emotion. Every rat killed mice placed in its cage. They also noted that the drug-induced killing had the same appearance as a natural killing; that is, the kill was made with a bite through the cervical spinal cord even though the animals had neither killed before nor had seen other rats kill. When the scientists reversed the process, by injecting the killer rats with a substance that blocked the action of the brain chemical mimicked by carbachol, mice placed in the cages of the killers were sniffed at and stalked but were not attacked. An experiment like this raises the possibility that drugs may one day be used to treat human aggressors.

Chromosomes may also be implicated in violent behavior, as they are in Mongolism. Sex is determined by two chromosomes, X and Y. Normally, the female complement is XX, the male XY. But in every 500 male births, the complement is XXY rather than XY, with the error toward femaleness. If there is an error in the opposite direction, XYY, the resulting situation is often referred to as supermaleness. Unusually tall and somewhat retarded, this individual is found once in every 2,000 male adults. He may be more aggressive than normal males because of the extra bit of chemical information he carries. Many scientists believe that there is a definite link between the extra chromosome and emotional disturbance and criminal behavior, and that the XYY individual is more vulnerable to poor environmental influences than the XY male. This point is debated, however, particularly in the courts when a defense attorney seizes upon the abnormality in an effort to get his client acquitted.

Goodbye to Bedlam

Many controversial issues are raised by the ability of scientists to switch anger on and off — by radio waves that destroy tiny pieces of brain tissue at the site of "storms" and that stop seizures and relieve pain, and by drugs and neurological surgery to control aggressive behavior.

In the chapter on schizophrenia, an allusion was made to lobotomy, which refers to the cutting out of pieces of the brain's higher parts to improve behavior. The advent of tranquilizers pushed lobotomy into a back seat, but recently there has been a revival of the technique. "Without quite agreeing about the exact bodily location of the mind's strong impulses, surgeons are currently cutting, burning, irradiating, and electrifying various portions of the human brain — fortunately with techniques less imprecise than those that won earlier surgical 'soul-tamperers' the reputation of swinging ice picks indiscriminately across nerve fibers of people's frontal lobes," *Medical World News* commented in a recent report on lobotomy.

The issue of whether neurosurgery ought to be used to control violent behavior erupted at a 1972 neurological symposium on violence and aggression in Houston. At the meeting, a Washington, D.C., psychiatrist, Dr. Peter R. Breggin, a member of the Medical Committee for Human Rights, questioned the ethics and motives of some neurosurgeons and criticized the work of Dr. Ervin and Dr. Mark as well as what he called their "immense conclusion" that an early-warning system is needed "to screen God knows how much of the nation, and then possibly subject many to psychosurgery." To that he added, "We are currently in the midst of an enormous resurgence of psychosurgery in the United States and around the world. I've come across about 1,000 cases in the literature, and I have estimates of perhaps 400 to 600 operations a year, going on right here in the United States. But this is really just a beginning." Dr. Breggin, whose attack on psychosurgery was printed in the *Congressional Record* of February 24, 1972, said brain operations designed to control behavior were being performed even though they have little demonstrable value, and that they were being done on people with relatively intact personalities "solely for the purpose of making them less aggressive." Furthermore, he charged, many of the operations are being performed on hyperactive children, some only five years old, with neurotic women in their middle years the largest group undergoing such surgery.

At the same meeting, Dr. Mark issued a statement that noted, "Our patients who are candidates for temporal lobe electrodes are all temporal lobe epileptics with aggressive behavior or intractable fear. They have had a long trial period with antiepileptic and psychotherapy drugs, together with all forms of psychotherapy appropriate in these cases — without any success. . . . In a wider context, our group is surveying a group of patients with both focal brain disease and behavioral abnormalities of the episodic variety, especially violent behavior. We are not looking at these patients as surgical candidates, but are seeking to apply other kinds of treatment, that is, medical and psychiatric, to their problem — if a substantial link can be proven between their brain abnormality and their behavioral disorder. Our surgical approach has been restricted to episodically violent patients with intractable temporal lobe epilepsy who are over the age of 18." Both he and Dr. Ervin emphasized that they do not operate on patients who are not able to comprehend the operation, adding that all are private patients who volunteer and who are operated on only after intensive evaluation and after a group of physicians oversees the selection.

At a later neurological meeting in Boston, medical students and other protesters, calling themselves "People Against Psychosurgery," picketed and demanded that the doctors halt psychosurgery, which they characterized as "destruction of the brain to control behavior." The description drew a retort from Dr. H. Thomas Ballantine, a Massachusetts General Hospital neurosurgeon, who suggested that even the name psychosurgery is a misnomer. "We are operating on the brain, not the psyche," he said. "You can't operate on a psyche." In answer to Dr. Breggin's charge that the aim of the surgery is to pacify potential radicals, among other people, Dr. Ballantine added that the operation is designed to alleviate functional brain disorders.

In July of 1973, the National Association for Mental Health released a statement on psychosurgery, saying that it should not be used except where the patient is in such great emotional stress due to his mental disorder that he, by his own choice, would prefer such treatment rather than to remain with his existing condition. "Even though psychosurgery has proved beneficial in some cases," said Mrs. J. Skelly Wright, president of the association, "so little is known about the causes of mental disorders and the specific functioning of the brain that no consensus has yet been achieved within the medical profession concerning the effectiveness of this form of treatment. Because psychosurgery is still, to a large extent, experimental, it is absolutely essential that there be safeguards to protect patients who might otherwise be used as human guinea pigs." The association position advised that psychosurgery be regarded as a last resort, to be considered only when all other alternatives have been given adequate trial in the opinion of the patient, his family and at least two reputable physicians, one of whom should be a psychiatrist.

Since birth is a relatively dangerous event it has been suggested that everyone of us has a touch of mental retardation or some other defect as a result of slight brain damage at birth. "For the fetus," says Dr. Abraham Towbin, a physician at the Danvers (Massachusetts) State Hospital, "hypoxic and mechanical injury to the central nervous system, in some measure, is inescapable. Severe birth injury is a particularly imminent threat to the premature." Lack of oxygen, or hypoxia, is of major importance as a cause of chronic neurological disorder, he reported recently in the *Journal of the American Medical Association,* noting that severe hypoxia may result in mental retardation, cerebral palsy, or epilepsy. Mild hypoxia can result in minimal or latent symptoms of minimal brain dysfunction. It was Dr. Towbin's estimate that over three million Americans, adults as well as children, suffer from minimal brain dysfunction, a syndrome that affects many who have behavioral disorders and is often accompanied by learning defects, reading difficulty, hyperactivity, and inordinate awkwardness. Minimal brain damage, Dr. Towbin said, may reduce a child's potential from that of genius to that of an average child or less, or it may spell the difference between brothers, one a skilled athlete and the other an "awkward child." He also noted the high incidence of prematurity and other birth complications among older children and young adults with behavioral disturbances, dropouts, and delinquents, and said it was evident that adults, even in later years, may continue to show the effects of brain scarring incurred at birth.

A study at the University of Rhode Island suggested also that a significant percentage of so-called juvenile delinquents may actually suffer from subtle brain disorders. Using a battery of tests designed to detect these neurological disorders, Dr. Allan Berman, assistant professor of psychology, found that 17 out of 30 delinquent boys in a randomly chosen sample evidenced brain upset. "The delinquents we studied showed a wide range of neurological disorders," he reported to a conference of the Association of Children with Learning Disabilities in 1972. "Individual youngsters had difficulties using the information from their senses of sight, hearing or touch. Some showed difficulties in forming concepts, and some in sensing and controlling body movement. Our data indicate, interestingly, that many of the specific kinds of deficits from which the delinquents suffered were the same kinds of deficits encountered in nondelinquent children with learning disabilities." This finding raises the possibility that the only difference between the learning-disabled child and a delinquent is that the former has been diagnosed properly. "Such a child in whom the disability has been early and accurately diagnosed may be exposed to less frustration in school," Dr. Berman said. "Other neurologically impaired children, however, principally those in the lower class where proper diagnosis is unavailable, go unnoticed. Their school lives are filled with inadequacy, humiliation before family and peers and continued reinforcement of the feeling that school is a painful, unpleasant place." These children, the psychologist declared, become behavior problems, drop out of school, or are truant, and begin the inevitable road to delinquency.

Dr. Berman cautioned that the intent of his research was not to deny the existence or importance of emotional problems in delinquents. "Obviously a large number of delinquents have such problems," he said, "and many of them are neurologically normal. But it also is becoming apparent that in many other delinquents, brain disorders exist which lead to behavior problems. We believe that labeling these youngsters delinquents has resulted in a tragic mismanagement of their problem. If they could be thought of as children with specific learning problems, perhaps we would be more willing to try techniques which have proven successful in remedying these kinds of disabilities."

The time may have come for society to reexamine its attitudes toward delinquents and their treatment in the light of scientific findings that many people who are difficult to control and whose behavior runs counter to accepted standards may have motor difficulties that are part of their problem.

However, controls are necessary to guard against the unwarranted and careless use of treatments like psychosurgery, electrical brain stimulation, and drugs, for they are two-edged swords that can damage the brain as well as help it.

8 Therapies

There are many ways of treating mental illness, some of which have already been discussed. Since there are so many causes and so many kinds of mental disease it would be wrong to praise one form of therapy over another. Indeed, it is often a combination of several forms of therapy that is most helpful.

Both psychiatrists and psychologists deal with mental and emotional disorders, but their titles should not be confused. The American Psychiatric Association defines psychiatry as the medical science "which deals with the origin, diagnosis, prevention and treatment of mental and emotional disorders." This definition also includes such special fields as mental retardation, the emotional components of physical disorders, mental hospital administration, and the legal aspects of psychiatric disorders. Psychology may be defined as an academic discipline, a profession, a science dealing with the study of mental processes and behavior in man and animal. A psychiatrist is a doctor of medicine, an M.D., with specialized training and experience in mental and emotional disorders. A psychologist, who specializes in psychology, usually holds a Ph.D. or M.A. degree. There is another title, that of clinical psychologist, usually a psychologist with a Ph.D. who has had further training in a medical setting and who specializes in research and/or diagnosis and psychotherapy in the field of mental and emotional disorders. Psychiatrists and psychologists often work together, though occasionally the two professions are at odds over which one is better qualified to deal with mind disorders.

The term "psychotherapy" commonly refers to any of several treatments in which a trained therapist uses verbal or nonverbal communication in an attempt to normalize a patient's abnormal behavior. Different from therapies that focus on the physical, such as drugs, shock, and surgery, psychotherapy tries to reform the disordered mind by helping the patient understand why he behaves as he does. The doctor talks to the patient and gives him an opportunity to let his troubles out — often the best way to deal with relatively mild depressions and neuroses. Sometimes the simple act of ventilation (talking out of problems) coupled with reassurance from the therapist are enough to help the patient. At other times a more intense, more probing kind of psychotherapy is required, psychoanalysis. The founder of this method of studying past and present emotional problems was the noted Austrian neurologist Sigmund Freud (1856–1939), whose work and theories have influenced many psychiatrists but which are also responsible for a number of opposing schools of thought. Some of these dissident views will be examined later.

Psychoanalysis, a theory of human psychological development as well as a method of treatment, is based on the idea that mental abnormality stems from our repressed and unconscious inner conflicts. Freud's theories form the foundation of what is known as dynamic psychiatry, the study of motives that emphasizes the changes and exchanges of energy that take place inside the personality. The physical counterpart of this theory is dynamics, the mechanical branch of physics that deals with the motion and equilibrium of systems that are acted upon by forces, usually from outside the system. Descriptive psychiatry, on the other hand, is an older system dealing with the study of easily observable external factors, symptoms, and classifications of mental illnesses. Freud underwent an intense self-analysis, delving deeply into his unconscious. He analyzed his dreams and those of his patients, and concluded that they were associated with conscious and unconscious desires, that they were a gateway to the mind and its hidden motivations. He concentrated a good deal on psychosexual developments, on instinctual drives that go back to early childhood, and he gave us the id, the ego, the superego, and the Oedipus complex. With his patients lying relaxed on a couch, Freud let them talk, pour out their innermost thoughts, emotions, and desires, say whatever came into their minds — what he called free association — while he analyzed and interpreted what they told him. Through this technique, all that is hidden by a person surfaces, helping him to better understand his motivations and his entire being. By putting himself on display, as it were, by talking honestly about himself, the patient hopefully will know more about himself than he ever knew, or would admit to knowing, before. Armed with this insight, he then can go on to restructure his thinking so that he can live more comfortably and realistically, and be less hung up by irrational guilt and anxiety. The role of the analyst in this form of therapy is that of a helper, an interpreter, not that of an authoritative instructor who snaps orders and gives advice to someone who lies obediently on a couch without expressing himself.

There are non-Freudian forms of analysis, among which are the schools of Carl Gustav Jung, Alfred Adler, and Otto Rank.

Jung, who died in 1961, founded the school of analytic psychology, a system that places less emphasis on sexual factors in psychoneuroses than Freud's does. While he was an early pupil of Freud and applied much of his teacher's ideas to his own work, Jung decided that the libido was not exclusively a sexual drive but, rather, a creative force and a natural energy that spurred all human conduct, a mix of every impulse and instinct of the mind. For Jung, the unconscious contained attitudes inherited from our ancestors, a collective racial consciousness, as well as individual experiences. He also classified people as extroverts and introverts, individuals who are, respectively, outgoing and interested in people and events outside themselves, and those who are preoccupied with themselves.

Adler, an Austrian psychologist who also studied with Freud, similarly rejected Freud's view of the libido as primarily sexual. It was his idea that early in life man acquires an "inferiority complex," a feeling of inadequacy that causes anxiety or timidity and forces the individual to compensate by becoming overly ambitious or aggressive. It is, therefore, not the sexual drive that is at the heart of mental upset but the struggle between man's burning desire for power and the feeling of inferiority that is with us from the moment we realize that there are others who are not as weak as ourselves. When the mechanisms we use to compensate get out of control, various neuroses and psychoses result.

Rank, another Austrian analyst who studied under Freud and became his secretary, theorized that neuroses were linked to the trauma of birth. He deemphasized the Oedipus complex and believed that the ego was submissive to the id. Rank also advocated less rigidity in analytic treatment, preferring a more active relationship between analyst and patient and concerning himself more with the patient's problems of the moment than on dredging up the past, as Freud did.

Several American analysts have left their mark on psychoanalytic theory, among them Karen Horney, Erich Fromm, and Henry Stack Sullivan. These three stressed social, cultural, and interpersonal factors instead of the purely Freudian idea of man as an island unto himself, an individual who is constantly at war with his instincts.

Horney, who died in 1952, spurned Freud's libido theory, deemphasized early psychosexual growth and genetic factors, and stressed environmental and cultural elements in her theory of neurosis. Some neuroses, she believed, sprang from the anxiety hinging on a single conflict in a person's environment. They prevented a person from functioning systematically, but did not run deep. Other neuroses, Horney said, were rooted in a basic anxiety that resulted from a childhood devoid of fondness and love. She called the first of these situation neuroses, the latter character neuroses.

Fromm, who applied psychoanalytic theory to cultural

and social problems, did not see instinct or biological factors as man's prime movers. Rather, he believed that what was all-important were "specific kinds of a person's relatedness to the world"; that is, certain personality types are related to specific socioeconomic patterns, that our behavior is determined by culture. In one of his principal works, *Escape from Freedom* (1941), Fromm wrote that the drives that make for the difference in a man's character, such as love, hate, lust for power, the enjoyment and the fear of sensuous pleasure, are "products of the social process," not a biological mold, that our needs are determined largely by the society in which we live. Fromm did not deny that man's behavior is spurred by biological signals, but he did believe that society's demands envelop those of the instinct or libido, making them less important.

Sullivan, who was director of the Washington (D.C.) School of Psychiatry from 1936 to 1947, is best known for his theory of interpersonal relations, which states that a person's character development, behavior, mental disorders, and neurotic symptoms are all the result of his interaction with others and with social forces.

Not every psychiatrist is an analyst. Those who wish to pursue this approach must be especially trained after they have finished their regular psychiatric education. Psychoanalysis has come in for much criticism lately and often at the hands of psychiatrists themselves. There are many who wonder about its worth, pointing out that it is by no means a cure for every mental problem because there are so many problems and because each person is unique. Psychoanalysis is a time-consuming method of treatment, often requiring months and even years of application. And it is costly — $25 and more a half hour. Then, too, many patients are unable to withstand the relentless pursuit of the core of their troubles. The systematic process that puts one's psyche under a microscope and lays bare every fear, guilt, and desire, dissects each one, and then tries to put them together again may be too much for some people. Often, the restructuring process may be like trying to patch up Humpty Dumpty.

A survey done a few years ago by the National Institute of Mental Health determined that analysis was the least used of nearly fifty recognized forms of psychiatric therapy in the United States. A more recent study presented at an annual meeting of the American Psychiatric Association also showed that the classical analytical technique introduced by Freud more than seventy years ago plays a small part in today's psychiatric practice. The study, by the U.S. Public Health Service, found that only 2 percent of some 55,000 patients under treatment by 333 psychiatrists in private practice were in Freudian analysis. About 4 percent were involved in group therapy, and the rest were undergoing individual consultation without intensive analysis.

"Freud felt that a patient had to be opened up to find the unconscious scars and then painstakingly knit together better than before," Dr. Lewis Wolberg, head of New York's Postgraduate Center for Mental Health, has said. "We think the patient should be practically helped to reconstruct his personality as far as he can go. We do not feel it is necessary to tear the whole building down. It is often more advantageous and practical to repair it. A leaky roof is very easy to repair provided the foundation is solid. As far as the role of the analyst is concerned, research studies show that patients get better where the therapist displays empathy, understanding, and 'care' about the patient."

Another dissenter, one of the most controversial figures in psychiatry today, is Dr. Thomas Szasz, a psychoanalyst and professor of psychiatry at the Upstate Medical Center in Syracuse. "Psychoanalysis is vanishing," he was quoted as saying in the *New York Times* in 1968. "It is as moribund and irrelevant as the Liberal Party in England." The author of numerous books and articles on what he calls the myth of mental illness and on the menaces of psychiatry, Dr. Szasz is deeply concerned over the threat the mental health movement poses for individual rights. Some of his views will be summarized in the concluding chapter.

Others contend that psychoanalysis has not been scientifically proved effective, that other less costly and less drawn-out methods, including religion, have brought as good, if not better results, that it has not come up with any significant discoveries or breakthroughs in recent times, that it is a "horse-and-buggy" approach that can only be afforded by patients with money. The critics charge also that analysts are too dogmatic about right and wrong behavior, that the analyst's detached approach further alienates the patient, who would be better served if the therapist advised him.

One form of therapy attempts to do just that. It is called supportive psychotherapy, and it involves the therapist's use of a number of measures, such as advice, reassurance, persuasion, reeducation, suggestion, and inspiration. Supportive psychotherapy buttresses a patient's mental defense mechanisms, does not delve too deeply

127

into a psyche that may not be strong enough to hold up under the probing, and helps the patient suppress things that might be disturbing to him.

Another widely used form of therapy involves the group. The product of a World War II shortage of trained personnel to treat psychiatric patients, group therapy enables an emotionally troubled individual to identify with others who have similar problems. By meeting regularly in a group with a psychiatrist or a psychologist, a disturbed person may slowly understand his own troubles as he listens to others discuss and share theirs. This method also has the advantage of costing less than individual therapy, and it can often benefit people who cannot be helped as effectively in other ways.

"Most persons who can be helped by psychotherapy can be helped either individually or through a group," says Dr. Leonard Horwitz, director of the Group Psychotherapy Service at the Menninger Foundation. "Some are better off in a group than in individual work and vice versa. If a person is very depressed, possibly suicidal, for example, he should be seen individually." A recent report from the foundation noted that its therapeutic groups are long-term ones, the objective being that a person find out more about himself and his relationships not only outside the group but also within it. Also, patients are not pressured to "open up" too quickly. They find support within the group first, then loosen up at their own pace. Often a soothing word, a touch of the hand, or a pat on the cheek are good beginnings.

Group therapy may be used to treat a variety of mental disorders and problems relating to alcohol and drug addiction. At Duke University Medical Center, Dr. John B.

Reckless, who heads the division of psychosomatic medicine, uses it to treat a strange form of conversion reaction in which persons develop what are called blepharospasms, the involuntary closing of the eyes. These patients have to be hospitalized, and their disability can become so severe — when their eyes are eventually closed more than open — that they must be declared legally blind. Often a patient realizes that certain events bring on the conversion reaction and he tries to avoid them. At Duke, blepharospasms were induced in one girl when her home situation was discussed in a group. When her eyes began to close, group members would ask her what she was thinking about. Thus, by focusing attention on the thing that was bothering her, she could recognize what started the conversion reaction and watch for it. In other group sessions some patients are given bells, and whenever a person notices pain he rings the bell. The group then directs its attention to that particular patient, asking the location of the pain and why it hurts. The point of this approach is to help patients recognize why they react to pain that may have no physical basis.

Another way Dr. Reckless deconditions psychosomatic illness verbally is exemplified in the case of a young boy with asthma. The youth would begin to wheeze and cough whenever the group spoke of his father, but as the conversation shifted from the father the boy's eyes cleared and the asthma attack subsided. As soon as his father was mentioned again, the attack returned. Explains Dr. Reckless, "This boy was reacting to a conditioned response. It was possible to reverse the psychological, conditioned response and trace the source of the conditioned stimulus." (A conditioned response is one that comes about when something is repeated in association with a previously unrelated stimulus. The classic example is the dog experiment of Ivan Pavlov, 1849–1936, a Russian neurophysiologist noted for his work in the field of conditioned reflexes and who was awarded the Nobel prize in medicine in 1904 for his contributions to the physiology of digestion. Since dogs — and humans — salivate at the mention, sight, or taste of food, Pavlov decided to look into the mechanism behind the mouth-watering process. In his experiments, the animals were repeatedly offered food while a bell was rung. The dogs salivated at the sight of the food. Pavlov kept it up for a while, ringing the bell every time he gave his dogs food. After a time, he found that merely ringing the bell alone, with no food offered, made the dogs salivate. The bell was the conditioned stimulus, the salivation the conditioned response. Earlier, Pavlov had demonstrated that the stomach secreted gastric juice the moment food was placed on a dog's tongue.)

Adolescents often are helped by group therapy, according to the Menninger's Dr. Horwitz, because they are more influenced by a peer group. This is also true for those people plagued by shyness, stage fright, and unusual degrees of embarrassment. The group gives them a chance to air their phobias in a social environment.

Group therapy has also been used successfully to help patients who must undergo the trying experience of dialysis, a technique that has helped prolong the life of many people stricken with chronic kidney disease. Dialysis involves passing the patient's blood through a machine, or artificial kidney, in order to wash out various poisonous substances that normally functioning kidneys remove. Some 30,000 people in the United States die each year because they cannot afford hospital treatment and because they cannot handle often complex equipment at home. In severe cases of kidney disease a transplant may be required, and the patient is kept alive on a dialysis machine until a suitable donor is found. Dialysis requires that the patient virtually live with the machine from 6 to 14 hours two or three times a week.

Sometimes this routine becomes a strain and, with the constant threat of death hanging over him, the patient may become depressed, suicidal, and unwilling to cooperate. A few years ago, the Rockford Memorial Hospital Dialysis Center in Rockford, Illinois, designed a program to help patients with psychosocial problems. Noting that dialysis patients can help each other, the hospital started a group therapy program and held monthly meetings with twenty to forty people in attendance. All patients with terminal kidney failure who were scheduled to undergo dialysis or transplantation were invited, along with their spouses and other family members. The group included patients maintaining themselves on home dialysis as well as those linked to artificial kidneys in the hospital. Various members of the dialysis team — nurses, technicians, dieticians, psychologists, social workers, chaplains and physicians — also attended. The team is present, Dr. Ewald T. Sorensen reported in the *Journal of the American Medical Association,* not so much to furnish answers "as to set a milieu in which patients can learn to open up to each other and support each other through discussion of their mutual problems." The patients themselves are often asked to answer technical questions whenever possible, thereby strengthening their confidence in themselves and making them feel that they are helping the group. "The group situation has become a prime teaching technique since participants seem to learn faster from peers than from professionals," Dr. Sorensen explained. "A significant part of home dialysis training is the preparation of the patient to cope with such complications as coil leaks and machine failures. Several centers use mockups of machine complications for such teaching. One of our patients had a power failure caused by a storm during his first dialysis run at home. At the next group meeting he and his wife described vividly what happened and how they handled the situation. This greatly impressed the others there. When the next power failure occurred for another patient a few months later, his wife calmly cranked the machine by hand, and the event hardly made a ripple in the group." The point is that teaching from personal experience is often more effective than a formal lecture. Dr. Sorensen concluded that the group meetings have done much to change the whole atmosphere of the dialysis unit toward a positive, confident note, and have served as an effective way to combat the usual social isolation and psychological denial that the dialysis patients often experience.

There are several variations on the group therapy theme, one of which is the controversial sensitivity session, known also as the encounter group, the T-group (T for training), confrontation, or human potential laboratory. A typical session is a free-wheeling, "let-it-all-hang-out" discussion of each participant's failings and finer points. Unbridled self-expression is encouraged, whether it be screaming, bitterly denouncing one's own faults or those of someone else, or touching one another's faces. Mixed nude bathing, the most disputed therapy variant, plays a part in some programs, the idea being that if a person removes his clothes in public he might also be able to remove the cover from some of his emotions. Participants in sensitivity sessions may shout at each other such emotions as "I can't stand the sight of you," or "You bug me." They may lie in a row on the floor and tell fairy tales; they may stand blindfolded in a circle and clasp hands, saying nothing; or they may crawl about on all fours, finally selecting "the person who turns you on," and then sit staring into his or her eyes for a half hour. "Feel free," "Don't think it, feel it," and "It's what's happening now" are remarks frequently heard at an encounter group. Not a form of psychoanalysis (encounter groups aren't meant for the mentally ill or neurotic individuals, although at times an emotionally disturbed person will gain admittance to a group run loosely by an unqualified director), the sensitivity session is designed to do just what the name implies, to stimulate sensitivity. Properly conducted, say its adherents, it breaks down communication barriers, enables people to get along better with other human beings, promotes honesty, understanding, sympathy, and concern for others, and enhances everyday performance.

More a learning than a therapeutic experience, sensitivity sessions are also seen as a way to "turn on and tune in" without drugs, and people from many walks of life are enrolled in encounter groups today. Even large corporations have sponsored sensitivity training programs for their employees, and many clergymen are in such programs in an effort to help them improve rapport with parishioners. School systems and police departments have also begun participating in encounter programs, and one estimate is that more than 25 million Americans have engaged in this method of "consciousness raising." But at the same time that the movement has caught on like wildfire, it has come in for its share of criticism. Some of the reaction is extreme, from superconservatives who are for motherhood, the flag, and good roads, and who violently oppose such things as sex education in the schools and fluoridation of the water supplies. For some of these people, sensitivity training is known disdainfully as "group grope" and dismissed as a form of Communist brainwashing aimed at undermining America's values. Other critics of a more reasonable sort express concern over amateur-run sensitivity sessions that may be psychologically damaging to some participants, particularly those who are emotionally disturbed to begin with. Not everyone should enroll in programs like this, for many are unable to survive the sometimes brutal ripping down of long-standing defenses, and, say the more responsible critics, too often people in need of real psychiatric assistance put off such help in favor of an encounter group that a newspaper advertisement has led them to believe is the answer to their problems. Others see it as practicing psychiatry without a license (some of the programs do use psychiatric techniques), and they question whether any long-term benefits accrue for the participants.

Says Dr. Dana L. Farnsworth, who has been director of the Harvard University Health Services and chairman of the American Medical Association's Council on Mental Health: "Sensitivity training can all too easily become insensitivity training. There can be great danger for the person who has psychotic difficulties or who is involved in any sort of acute crisis."

Recently, at an annual meeting of the American Group Psychotherapy Association, Dr. S. R. Slavson told the group, "Obviously, latent or borderline psychotics with tenuous ego controls and defenses may, under the stress of such groups and the complete giving up of defense, jump the barrier between sanity and insanity."

Still others, civil libertarians among them, are deeply distressed at sensitivity sessions that may be an invasion of privacy. A few years ago, several federal supervisors complained to Senator Sam J. Ervin, a North Carolina Democrat who heads the Senate Judiciary Subcommittee on Constitutional Rights, that they were obliged to participate in confrontation sessions that probed their thoughts on racial issues, the purpose being to improve the lot of blacks who applied for jobs. The senator charged that such a practice was oppressive, saying, "It subjects employees to a probe of their psyches, to provoke and indeed to require disclosure of their intimate attitudes and beliefs during emotionally charged situations."

Whether an encounter group is the educational breakthrough its devotees say it is, and whether what is learned (if anything) in three days of shouting, weeping, and embracing sticks after the participant walks out onto the street and back into his daily routine, remains to be seen. "For good or ill," said a report in the AMA's *Today's Health* magazine, "sensitivity training appears to be more than a passing fad. In its more bizarre forms, as a means of providing thrill seekers with a quick emotional jolt, it may fade into obscurity once the novelty has worn off and the publicity has subsided. But as a means of learning to cope in a group, of discovering and capitalizing upon hidden inner strengths its potential appears limitless."

Goodbye to Bedlam

Taking its cue from Pavlov, behavior therapy is another of the newer modes of treatment. It deemphasizes the unconscious and what lies in the patient's past, concentrating instead on his current behavior and problems. Known also as learning therapy, or conditioning therapy, the approach treats human beings somewhat like animals in the sense that they can be trained or taught to rid themselves of undesirable behavior. Neuroses and psychoses do not grow out of unconscious repression, the behavior therapist says, but are simply bad habits that the patient has somehow learned. Whereas the approach of the psychoanalyst is to attempt to bring about indirect changes in the patient's overt behavior by focusing on his subjective feelings and thoughts, the behavior therapist centers at once on his overt behavior. If you change the way a person acts, the behavior therapist believes, you may even change the way he thinks and feels, rather than the other way around.

Behavior therapists use different conditioning and desensitizing techniques to help the patient relearn and thus bring about desired behavior. A rather chilling exaggeration of behavior therapy appears in the Anthony Burgess novel and movie, *A Clockwork Orange*. The central character is Alex, a violent and guiltless individual who undergoes conditioning in order to cure his savage conduct. Bound tightly, with his eyes propped open, he is subjected to a barrage of films portraying all manner of violence until his former way of life becomes abhorrent to him and he is transformed into a paragon of virtue. However, in an ironic twist at the end, Alex reverts to his earlier frame of mind, made violent again by a "model" society.

Real methods, of course, are not so drastic. One way is to teach the patient to relax his muscles completely, thus setting up a defense against anxiety. The therapist then ties the relaxed condition to some situation that causes fear or anxiety, the aim being to make it harmless. He does this by asking the patient to imagine the weakest of several situations that have induced fear in the past at the same time he relaxes. The procedure is repeated several times — the fear is presented, the patient concentrates on relaxing — until the fear no longer evokes anxiety. Later, the patient is gradually exposed to stronger fear-producing situations as he relaxes, until those, too, can be tolerated. By being trained to relax when faced with a fearful situation or object, the patient reacts somewhat like Pavlov's dogs. The stimulus, in this case the fear, triggers a conditioned response, the relaxed state, which wipes out the phobia. If the therapy goes as it should, the patient will, when faced with an actual fearful situation, cope with it by making himself relax through concentration, associating his relaxed mood, which fights anxiety, with his phobia.

Another technique is to ask the patient to concentrate on some particularly disturbing and obsessive thought, one that he has discussed with the therapist. It may, for instance, be that he will die in his sleep. The patient thinks hard about the fear, and without warning the therapist shouts one word at him, "Stop!" The patient is startled, and the nagging thought is temporarily wiped out. He then is asked to talk about some of his fears, and when he mentions the fear of dying the therapist yells again, once more canceling the disturbing notion. After this is repeated in subsequent sessions, the patient learns to neutralize the offending thought without the therapist, simply by thinking "Stop!" whenever it appears. Later he may become so conditioned that the disturbing idea automatically orders its own end the moment it pops into his head.

Some behavior therapists use a method known as aversive therapy, or conditioned avoidance, in which electric shock or nausea-inducing drugs are associated with some objectionable impulse the patient is trying to shake. Alcoholics are often treated in this way, sometimes successfully. The chronic drinker may be given a drug to make him sick, and just before the nausea sets in an alcoholic beverage is placed before him. He links the subsequent sickness with the drink, and soon the thought as well as the sight of liquor is disgusting. An electric shock (not to be confused with electroconvulsive therapy, or electric shock treatment, which will be discussed later) may be applied in the same way and has been used to treat homosexuals and individuals in the grip of some sexual perversion. A jolt of electricity may be shot into someone of the latter ilk, say a fetishist, someone who gives special meaning to an inanimate object. This often may be an article of feminine clothing, which the male fetishist substitutes for the woman and thus is sexually stimulated. The current shocks the patient each time women's apparel is shown to him, and eventually he associates the two and develops an aversion to the article that formerly attracted him.

There is considerable disagreement over whether this method of treatment provides a permanent cure. Taken as a whole, behavior therapy, which has been effective in treating phobias, is a valuable weapon in psychiatry's storehouse. Dr. Joseph Wolpe of Temple University School of Medicine, one of the country's renowned behavior therapists, has reported that 90 percent of his patients are cured or improved. Behavior therapy also is cheaper because it takes less time. It does, however, raise the same moral issues posed in the discussion of psychosurgery. Behavior therapy could be used as a tool to control behavior, to mold a race of people, for example, who would do the bidding of those in power. As in many of man's discoveries and creations – the harnessing of nuclear power is a prime example – there is great potential for both good and evil in behavior therapy, and it is to be hoped that therapists will emphasize the positive, applying their knowledge to the things that will benefit mankind most.

Behavior therapy is not the only treatment that frightens some with the images it conjures up of George Orwell's *1984* and robots out of science fiction who do the bidding of their masters. Electroconvulsive therapy (ECT), widely used to treat depression, evokes a similar response. Misunderstood by most and equated with something out of a Frankenstein movie, shock therapy has suffered from bad publicity and lack of adequate knowledge, even by psychiatrists. Contrary to popular opinion, it is not a discredited procedure and, while it is controversial, it is a relatively safe treatment that can terminate an episode of depression very quickly.

Interest in the procedure was revived during the 1972 presidential campaign when Senator Thomas F. Eagleton, the Democratic vice-presidential nominee, disclosed that he had undergone shock treatment for nervous exhaustion and depression. Eagleton later stepped down as a candidate but the episode touched off much debate, not only over the value of shock therapy but also whether a history of emotional distress should disqualify one from holding a high public office. The American Psychiatric Association issued a statement during the Eagleton affair, saying that shock has been a highly effective treatment for moderate and severe depression since it was introduced in 1938, and can often end depression in a matter of days, virtually always within a month. "In carefully selected cases for an episode of depression," the APA said, "electroshock treatment has proven approximately 90 percent effective." The association went on to note that in the past decade a variety of antidepressant drugs had become available and were frequently used in cases that would formerly have received ECT. Often, it pointed out, the drugs are very effective, but in general their effectiveness is variable. They can be easily administered on an outpatient basis, but since response to them may take longer and is less predictable than in the case of shock, psychiatrists may choose the latter treatment, especially in the severe forms. "Shock is absolutely not a cure for a disorder," says Dr. Robert Arnot, a Boston psychiatrist who has used the treatment extensively. "But it gets rid of the 'sick' phase. I believe in getting rid of an illness, and then going on to why the person gets sick. Drugs probably will treat half of the patients we formerly used ECT on. And the doctors who give shock are those who have the most experience with drugs, and they know which ones won't work. There is a time factor involved in treating a disorder of the mind. Sometimes just talking will do it, and there is a time when sedation will do it, and a later time when shock therapy is needed."

Shock has been markedly successful in treating manic-depressive illnesses and, according to those who use it, corrects both phases of the disorder. Scientists have generally claimed that no one really knows why the passage of electric current through the brain works to alleviate depression. We do know, however, that the brain is an electrical instrument, and when its current misfires abnormal behavior results. Some scientists feel that electric current alters the brain's chemistry and thereby emotions. Dr. Arnot feels that it stimulates or changes the "setting" of the hypothalamus, the section of the brain that is the seat of emotions such as anger and fear. Others believe that shock works on memory molecules, blocking the upsetting thoughts that cause depression. Still others feel that shock scares a patient into getting better because he wishes to avoid another round.

In a standard ECT treatment, the patient is given medication to put him to sleep and another to relax his muscles. Then electrodes are taped to a patient's temples and a 110-volt current is passed into his brain. The current is applied for a few seconds; 10 to 12 treatments often are required. (In schizophrenia, more treatments are necessary, possibly 13 to 15 to begin and then one a month for a while.) As a result of ECT temporary amnesia occurs, a reaction that some psychiatrists believe could develop into a permanent memory gap if too many treatments are given.

While shock has been somewhat deemphasized since the introduction of various drugs in 1955, most psychiatrists do consider it a last-ditch effort to be used after psychotherapy and medication have failed to help. And many agree that it is clearly the method of choice for treating certain disorders, almost as specific in manic-depressive problems as penicillin is for an abscess. "When you have someone runnning a big business or is the head of a family whose absence or disability will be catastrophic," commented one state hospital psychiatrist, "it does become reasonable to give shock treatment rather than wait for the longer period of time it takes for drugs to become effective."

As to whether shock therapy — and a history of depression — make a person unfit to hold a job or public office, Dr. Arnot says, "We don't believe that shock disqualifies a person for anything. The only thing it does do is stimulate an interference with recent memory. A little piece of time is wiped out, like a blackboard drawing. It does not interfere with his performance, and he can even teach physics if he wants. What is important is how well the patient is doing now."

Insofar as depression is concerned, the APA has pointed out that during such an episode a person's judgment may be affected in proportion to the degree of depression. The distortion of judgment may vary from a slight coloration to a gross defect, but following recovery from the bout there is a full return of judgmental capacity. "In general, the assumption of normal activities by countless thousands of people who have been successfully treated for depression is compelling evidence that the existence of an episode of depression in a person's medical history should be considered in the same manner as a wide range of other successfully treated illnesses," said the APA.

Hypnosis is sometimes employed in a therapeutic program, and it, too, can effectively remove certain symptoms. But, like shock, it is not a cure, and it does not

142

attack the root of the illness. It treats the symptoms, not the sickness, and allows the patient to become open to suggestion. Long used for the relief of pain by dentists and physicians, hypnosis has been effectively applied in the cases of obese patients, alcoholics, addicts, smokers, in the treatment of psychosomatic skin disorders, and in changing the attitudes of elderly patients toward nursing homes to help them adjust easier. Ulcer patients may also be treated with hypnotherapy; for example, the physician may induce the sufferer to accept a suggestion that the vagus nerve is a wire stretched between the brain and the stomach, and that he can mentally disconnect this wire to cut down the acid flow. In one study, an analysis of stomach contents showed that there was a marked decrease in the level of hydrochloric acid with the subsequent loss of symptoms in more than 75 percent of the hypnotized patients.

Hypnosis has also been described as a means of inducing "conditioned self-control" and enhancing an individual's intellectual potential. Dr. Gaetano Piserchia, who taught a course in medical hypnosis for doctors at the Institute of Psychologic Studies in Milan, has attached much importance to this. According to a 1966 report in *Medical Tribune,* the doctors who take Dr. Piserchia's course are taught the mechanism of conditioned self-control, which, if taken to its extreme, can enable the patient or physician to alter his own heart and basal metabolic rate. "This has obvious implications for sports medicine," said Dr. Piserchia. "Athletes can be 'doped' by hypnosis to draw on otherwise untapped physical and mental resources. The physically handicapped can be taught to teach themselves how to achieve optimal muscular coordination and to apply the principles of isometric exercises with the minimum expenditure of time and energy."

Although hypnosis has a definite place in psychiatry and medicine, it can be dangerous in the wrong hands — in parlor games, for instance — or even when it is improperly used by health professionals. Reporting in the *Journal of the American Medical Association* a few years ago, Dr. Louis J. West of the University of Oklahoma School of Medicine and Dr. Gordon H. Deckert of the Oklahoma City Veterans Administration Hospital noted that while the hypnotic trance itself is a virtually benign or harmless condition, the danger to the patient seems to come from his response to suggestion and his reaction to a situation as it appears to him. As an example, they cited a college girl who developed a severe anxiety hysteria when an amateur hypnotist at a party ordered her to cut off her hair with an imaginary scissors. The doctors said also that hypnosis carelessly used may bring on a psychiatric illness, may make existing mental conditions worse, or may revive symptoms of an illness that was improving. Another danger to the patient is that hypnosis may mask symptoms to such an extent that the patient appears to be healthy. He may even feel and act well, but hiding symptoms this way may delay necessary psychiatric treatment. Patients may also become dependent on the hypnotist, the report went on, or criminal activity may be induced (though experiments have given conflicting evidence). There are dangers to the hypnotist, too. "Because of his ability to induce hypnosis and thereby influence others," the doctors said, "the operator may become convinced that he is somehow superior to other people, or that he enjoys powers beyond the scope of ordinary men. . . . The process of such corruption may turn a well-meaning hypnotist, devoted to his work, into a grandiose professional cripple."

There are many other adjunct approaches to the treatment of mental illness, among which are industrial therapy and the use of art, dance, poetry, music, and drama. They are not to be construed as cures, and do not get at the underlying cause of the problem, but they often help when employed with other techniques.

One unique mode of industrial therapy has been underway for several years at the Brockton (Massachusetts) Veterans Administration Hospital. It involves a community-hospital-industry-rehabilitation program (CHIRP). Light assembly jobs are furnished by local industries for which the patients are paid. More than 250 industries in New England and some outside states provide work to be done at the hospital.

Art therapy encourages the patient to express himself spontaneously in pictures. As he paints or draws, he may symbolize unconscious ideas and conflicts, feelings that are known only to him and that he may have declined to communicate to anyone else. A skilled therapist does not try to interpret the artwork to the patient. Rather, he prompts the patient-artist to explain the pictures himself. If the therapist is successful, the patient will release some of his suppressed thoughts, which only intensive psychoanalysis might have freed, and leave clues to his behavior. Later, the therapist might discuss the symbolism in the artwork, pointing out that certain elements may stand for fear, guilt, or frustration, thus helping the patient better understand what troubles him. Not only does art therapy

145

bring out hidden emotion and stimulate the patient to talk about things he might have avoided, it is also relaxing and enjoyable, exerting the same calming effect on a mentally ill patient that it does on many who paint as a hobby.

Dance and movement therapy go back to such ancient systems as yoga and Tai-Chi Chuan, disciplines that weld mind and body for the purpose of attaining physical and mental control and well-being. Yoga, a school of Hindu philosophy, teaches the suppression of all activity of body, mind, and will so that the self may realize its distinction from them and be liberated. It uses a system of physical and mental exercises for achieving bodily and mental control. Tai-Chi Chuan, which began in China more than a thousand years ago, is a system of ritualistic exercises somewhat akin to shadowboxing, except that the movements of the arms and legs are slow and flowing. The mind is calm and concentrates only on the various movements, which remind one of swimming in air or slow-motion ballet, all of it designed to bring about "a synthesis of body and mind in harmony," as one practitioner has put it. Dance and movement therapy is both recreation and emotional catharsis, and has helped many emotionally disturbed individuals become freer, mentally and physically, as they act out fantasy and shed themselves of aggression, hostility, and anxiety as well as muscular tension. It has been described as the creation of emotional honesty through dance. Said one young man who found dance therapy a good thing; "I know it's changed my outlook. I used to be only half aware of things around me. Now I'm a radio, believe me."

Allowing patients to dramatize their emotional problems, to act them out verbally, is a technique of group psychotherapy known as psychodrama. Created by Dr. J. L. Moreno and introduced in the United States in 1925, psychodrama permits a patient to be actor and audience at the same time. The patient is the central character, the protagonist. Other persons, known as auxiliary egos, participate in the stage action; they may be former patients or people who come from an environment similar to that of the patient. These auxiliaries, extremely important in psychodrama, portray the central figure's perceptions of significant people in his private life, real and imagined, dramatizing his inner feelings and experiences so that he sees them more clearly. There may be a specially selected audience, chosen with respect to the particular problem presented by the protagonist. A director is present, usually the psychiatrist in charge of treatment. Drawing on what the patient has told him, the director assigns roles to the "actors" and generally oversees the production. Psychodrama, which encourages self-expression and promotes group interaction, is not play-acting in the usual sense, and is not meant to entertain. It has been used in the treatment of schizophrenics and homosexuals, among others, and several colleges and medical centers have employed it lately to help young people realize that death and dying are a part of life. By playing roles in dramas involving death, by experiencing it, so to speak, students take a closer look at it, even though it is not real, and thus soften their qualms about the subject.

Music also is used as therapy in many hospitals. Once more, such a path is not a cure for mental illness, but it does provide an outlet for patients, easing their tensions and frustrations and giving them a sense of accomplishment. Pianos, guitars, trumpets, and group singing are all part of the therapy that is used in a broad range of disorders, including mental retardation, autism, and geriatric problems. Even the casual playing or singing of a few notes or words can awaken the deepest sentiments — as occurred, for example, in this scene at Boston State Hospital. A young man, a music therapist, was playing a soft melody on a piano in a room of about thirty mentally ill men. "Oh, Danny boy, the pipes, the pipes are calling," he sang. The patients shuffled their feet, rustled their songbooks, and then slowly picked up the familiar lyrics. "From glen to glen and down the mountainside. The summer's gone and all the roses falling . . ." One man, old and silver-haired, was bent low in his chair, his elbows perched on his knees, his hands holding the songbook out of sight down near his ankles. He was not singing; his lips were pursed and there was a frown on his brow. But then, with the music all about him, he brightened suddenly, and sang with the rest, "It's I'll be there in sunshine or in shadow, Oh Danny boy, oh Danny boy, I love you so." When it was over, he announced, to no one in particular, "God, I love to sing. I'd sing all day if they'd let me."

It should be emphasized that music itself does not cure anything (the popular adage about the savage breast notwithstanding). But it does have value in its contribution to the total treatment program, and it can help the patient to a more effective adjustment to society and to better mental health.

In another direction, home treatment of the emotionally disturbed has proven successful in keeping patients out of the hospital, helping them before their emotional troubles explode into major crises. Sixteen years ago, Massachusetts became the first state in the nation to use "house calls" as a method of treating the mentally ill, from children to the very old. Some have physical problems. They may be bedridden, without transporatation, or without a baby-sitter. Others are too upset to get themselves to a clinic, and some are simply afraid that seeing a doctor will mean going to the hosptial. Others frequently visited include the families of retarded children and people who are withdrawn or depressed. "About 30 percent more of our patients could profit from home treatment techniques," according to the director of one outpatient clinic for the retarded. "Families who have hyperactive or destructive children with mixed diagnoses seem to profit more from home visitations."

That is also the goal of a new kind of "away-from-hospital" psychiatric treatment for young Vietnam-era veterans that shows great promise of preventing the long-term mental illness and prolonged hospitalization common in the past. Under sponsorship of the Veterans Administration, the program begins with a period of hospitalization for "crisis intervention" with medication and counseling. This is followed by psychological testing, after which patients move to one of several homelike settings. For some, it is an apartment on the hospital grounds where they receive group therapy. Others live in a VA-sponsored group residence in the community, where they attend mental health schools modeled after colleges. The new treatment is only for a select group, according to the VA's chief psychiatrist, Dr. Joseph Baker. Some do better in the hospital, and those whose level of functioning becomes unsatisfactory are brought back to the hospital. On the whole, however, the nonhospital treatment is working well.

The VA is also using satellite psychosocial clinics in some small towns, and in some states VA mental health workers live in small towns to coordinate resources for the veteran's benefit. The trend away from institutionalizing patients carries through to VA hospitals. In 1973, for example, there were 48 day treatment centers, 37 day hospitals and 80 mental hygiene clinics.

According to Dr. Baker, treatment for mental illness in the VA is showing the same rate of progress as treatment of tuberculosis showed two decades ago. "During the 1950s and 1960s, we had tremendous advances as the tranquilizers and other psychotropic drugs came into use," he says. "Now, we have other advances. Psychologists have utilized learning methods to reinforce behavior to speed the process of learning to cope with stress and to live more normally. A great deal is also being learned about brain waves. Mental health research indicates that treatment of schizophrenia is frequently a teaching and learning process and that schizophrenia need not lead to deterioration of intelligence. We know that the hospital is not the normal or best place to learn to live again, and in many cases we would not be doing a man a favor by keeping him in the hospital."

Finally, no discussion of therapies would be complete without mentioning a chemical treatment, lithium, one of the main ingredients of the hydrogen bomb (also used as a glaze in ceramics). An alkali metal discovered in 1817, lithium is the lightest of the solid elements. Some twenty years ago, investigators found that it showed great potential as a psychoactive drug, but only in the past few years have significant numbers of researchers turned their attention to it. Lithium is known to calm the manic stage of manic-depressive psychosis, and it has been suggested that lithium maintenance may guard against recurring attacks of both mania and depression, and may be useful in other mental disorders as well. Some researchers have found a relationship between mental hospital admissions and the amount of lithium in tap water; admissions tended to decrease in areas where lithium levels were high. An Australian physician, Dr. John F. J. Cade, was the first to use the drug on disturbed patients. He tried it on guinea pigs, then on himself. He reported that he used it on patients with manic excitement and found dramatic improvement in each one. Other investigators have recorded similar successes, and the U.S. Food and Drug Administration recently approved lithium salts for the treatment of manics. Just how lithium does its job in the treatment of mental disorder is not known, but it has been suggested that it cuts down the concentrations of the adrenal hormone, epinephrine, at receptor sites in the central nervous system, thereby reducing the supposed mood-elevating effect of the hormone that mediates transmission of sympathetic nerve impulses.

The success of lithium therapy demonstrates again, as in the chemical treatment of schizophrenia, that physical approaches to the treatment of mental illness have great merit. And in this is hope, for it means there is a weapon against an enemy that is as elusive and as shapeless as the wind. But because of this very character of mental illness, one would be well advised to think a bit before making any authoritative pronouncements favoring one cause over another, or one therapy over another. What is important is the aim of all therapy, physical or psychological, and that is to help the mentally ill patient live comfortably with himself and in society.

9 Conclusion

In the opening chapter, the question was raised, "Who are the mentally ill, and what is mental illness?" The answer, we found, is not easy to come by, and about all we can do is to fall back on the names and symptoms of a variety of disorders, some of which have been discussed here, whose causes are either physical, psychological, or a combination thereof, and that affect our behavior in such a way as to place it markedly out of the ordinary.

While mental illness may be difficult to define, what is certain is that since the Eagleton incident there has been a gratifying growth in public understanding and acceptance of emotional trouble. In fact, public opinion polls taken during the discussion of the senator's candidacy made it clear that the majority of the citizens surveyed indicated a positive attitude toward the capabilities of an individual who has received treatment for an emotional problem. At the same time, Irving H. Chase, president of the National Association for Mental Health, called on that majority to help educate those who continue to be influenced by the myths and misconceptions about mental illness and who still make up a significant minority.

Chase declared that he believed that it was concern for the size of the minority that clearly influenced the decision to have Senator Eagleton withdraw from the ticket. "The majority which has learned to view mental illness objectively and without fear should join ranks in an all-out effort to inform all Americans of the facts about mental illness," Chase said. "We must clear from all minds all unfair doubts and fears about mental illness so that soon everyone will be aware that with proper attention, mental illness should be treated like any other illness."

There are those, however, who carry those doubts and fears to extremes, and over the years campaigns characterizing such organizations as the National Association for Mental Health as Communist fronts have been waged by ultraconservative political groups. Among their specious arguments is one that mental health concerns have been planted by agents of communism or the radical left to demoralize Americans and spread defeatism. In a speech a few years ago, Senator Maurine Neuberger warned, "The successful efforts of these malignant groups to defeat badly needed mental health legislation focuses the potential danger of their campaign into sharp reality." She cited an instance in Wisconsin in which a "horde of John Birchers and other members of the radical right," all shouting that the mental health movement was a subversive plot, succeeded in beating twenty mental health measures that had seemed certain of passage. "Nor is the far right content with preventing public action," the Oregon senator declared. "The Daughters of the American

Revolution, in a publication, claimed that 80 percent of psychiatrists are 'foreigners, most of them educated in Russia.' To prove Moscow's 'complicity,' they are promoting a booklet called 'Brainwashing, a Synthesis of a Russian Textbook on Psychopolitics.' Further, as many of the names they point to are of Jewish origin, there is an unstated, but clearly implied anti-Semitism in their campaign."

Not all of the critics, however, are irresponsible ones. One of psychiatry's most outspoken and at the same time respected gadflies is Dr. Thomas Szasz, whose ideas about mental illness warrant much more space than is possible here. Basically, Dr. Szasz has charged that mental illness is not a disease that can be diagnosed, treated, and cured. He does not deny that people have mistaken or unusual ideas, experience disturbing or strange emotions, or exhibit "prohibited or stupid" behavior, all of which upset them as well as those around them. What he does deny is that such thought or conduct is best understood as a species of illness, or that it is best managed as "a problem in therapeutics." Rather, he regards these as problems of adjustment and communication, what he calls "problems in living." He believes that people who, because of their problems in living, seek out a psychotherapist do not suffer from a disease. "I also do not believe that the person who, because of his behavior, is committed to a mental hospital suffers from a disease, or that the effort to control his behavior in the interests of society is a species of treatment," he has said.

In a recent book, *The Manufacture of Madness,* he charges that as witches, heretics, and Jews were condemned to torture and death in the Middle Ages, so now are those guilty of behavioral heresy — actions that deviate from the norm — persecuted by involuntary confinement in mental institutions. "The belief in mental illness and the social actions to which it leads have the same moral implications and political consequences as had the belief in witchcraft," he writes. The doctor, he adds, has replaced the priest as Inquisitor in an age more scientifically than theologically inclined, demonstrating man's continuing need to seek out scapegoats to alleviate his anxieties. "Madmen" are manufactured by medical diagnoses, he believes, citing cases of persecution on the basis of political belief, race, religion, sexual attitudes, and economic status. "The point we must keep in mind is that in the days of demonology, if the physician could find no evidence of natural illness, he was expected to find evidence of withcraft; today, if he cannot diagnose organic illness, he is expected to diagnose mental illness. . . . Physicians have avoided and continue to avoid the conclusion that certain problems fall outside the scope of their expert knowledge and that they should therefore leave the person alone and unclassified, the master of his own fate."

In an address before the Church of Scientology Grand National Convention, in which he attacked institutional psychiatry and the mental health movement as enemies of freedom comparable to communism, Dr. Szasz declared, "The alliance between organized medicine and the American government is evil, not good; and, more particularly, that the alliance between organized psychiatry (or institutional psychiatry) and the American government has, under the guise of 'treating mental illness' actually produced a political apparatus for creating and persecuting deviance."

He added this thought-provoking comment:

Goodbye to Bedlam

Consider the sorts of things for which institutional psychiatry punishes the individual by means of stigmatization, incarceration and destruction of parts or all parts of his body: old age, especially when coupled with poverty: this is called "senile psychosis" (or some other fraudulent psychiatric diagnosic label); assuming the social role of the other sex: this is called "homosexuality" or "transvestism" and is considered both a disease and a crime; ingesting or injecting certain drugs prohibited by law: this is called "addiction" and is also considered both a disease and a crime; being tired of life and contemplating putting an end to it: this is called "psychotic depression" and is especially severely punished by psychiatrists; making certain false statements (like asserting that one is Jesus): this is called "schizophrenia," the most severe mental disease known to man. In short, institutional psychiatry either crassly defends the status quo, or ruthlessly promotes its own power and prestige. It is hardly surprising, then, that when the State lies, it is called "mental health information"; when the individual lies, it is called "schizophrenia." When the state administers methadone to prisoners who do not want it, it is called "rehabilitation" and "treatment"; when the individual takes methadone on his own initiative, it is called "addiction" and "drug abuse." When the State operates a lottery with very poor odds for those who wager, it is considered a "liberal" policy for enhancing the public welfare; when an individual operates a gambling enterprise with far better odds for those who wager, he is considered a criminal, and those who gamble are considered infantile psychopaths. And so on, down to the minutest nook and cranny of our contemporary society.

To those who object that such inconsistencies and hypocrisies have always been with us, that such things are "human nature," Dr. Szasz replies, "True enough. But they have not always been promoted and enforced by a profession recognized as a medical specialty, namely, institutional psychiatry."

With further reference to confinement in a mental institution, Dr. Szasz wrote recently in the *New England Journal of Medicine* that so-called voluntary mental hospitalization often is actually a "covert form" of involuntary hospitalization. Typically, it is a case of a person being forced to sign himself in as a voluntary patient under the threat of commitment, Dr. Szasz said, and when, having been admitted to the hospital as a "voluntary" patient, he is not unqualifiedly free to leave when he wishes. In support of his comment that voluntary mental patients are actually, or at least potentially, prisoners, the doctor cited a recent case in Utah involving a woman who admitted herself as a voluntary patient to the state hospital and died. The woman's heirs sued the hospital for her "wrongful death" and the hospital claimed immunity under the Governmental Immunity Act and was upheld by the Utah Supreme Court. Dr. Szasz said that the court's decision was based on what it regarded as the fundamental similarities between jail and a mental hospital when it stated, "We might suggest that a voluntary patient at the hospital is as much 'confined' and has as little protection as a mentally alert trusty in a jail or prison."

Commented Dr. Szasz, "In short, there is no such thing as voluntary hospitalization, nor can there be so long as there is involuntary mental hospitalization. If it is generally true that voluntary mental patients are, in effect, prisoners, present legal and psychiatric practices regarding voluntary mental hospitalization are nothing but strategies of entrapment: to avoid the inconvenience of involuntary hospitalization, increasing numbers of Americans are seduced or coerced into assuming the status of involuntary mental patient 'voluntarily.'" He added that if mental hospital patients, even voluntary ones, have as little freedom as a trusty, it follows that psychiatrists who confine such persons in mental hospitals "behave like jailers, not like doctors." This, he concluded, confronts university administrators and medical and psychiatric educators with a moral dilemma: Are medical schools and psychiatric residency programs the appropriate institutions in our society for the training of jailers and wardens?

In a companion article in the journal, Dr. Milton Greenblatt, Massachusetts Mental Health Commissioner, and Dr. A. Louis McGarry replied that the continuation of the practice of voluntary mental hospital admission "under certain contractual conditions" is a desirable alternative to court-mediated involuntary commitment. They said also that though Dr. Szasz challenges the practice of conditional voluntary mental hospital admission, his main attack is on the social policy that authorizes involuntary mental hospital admission, and he favors its total abolition. They added, "Many people of good will and good intentions are being misled by this simplistic approach to public policy. Total abolition of involuntary civil commitment of the mentally ill is likely to be regressive, leading to an increased use of the criminal justice system in the management of the mentally ill, with destructive consequences. There will probably always be some citizens who require conditional voluntary or involuntary commitment status in mental health facilities." They reported also that the greatest pressures on them as officials of the state mental health department came from family members and the community to admit and retain the mentally ill and retarded. "Our sharpest and angriest critics among practicing legal and medical professionals and the citizenry are those who are convinced that we deny admission too frequently, that we discharge patients too soon and that we do not pursue patients who leave our hospitals without authorization," they said.

Whether mental illness is indeed a myth is an interesting question to ponder, even though the vast majority of those working in the medical and scientific fields feel otherwise. What has been attempted here is a description of some of the categories of mental disturbance, their causes and their treatment. The emphasis has been not only on the belief that these disorders are real ones, but also on the fact that while a schizophrenic in Akron might behave exactly like a schizophrenic in Madrid, or a retarded child in New York the same as a retarded child in New Zealand, the origins of these and the other problems discussed are still under study, the treatments are varied, and that phrases like "mental illness" and "mental health" are by no means definitive.

In conclusion, consider that latter phrase, mental health, an easy pair of words that is thrown about so casually and that seems to mean simply the absence of mental illness. The American Psychiatric Association defines mental health as "a state of being which is relative rather than absolute, in which a person has effected a reasonably satisfactory integration of his instinctual drives. His integration is acceptable to himself and to his social milieu as reflected in his interpersonal relationships, his level of satisfaction in living, his actual achievement, his flexibility, and the level of maturity he has attained."

The American Medical Association sees it this way: "Sound mental health means that a person is assuming the responsibilities that a person of his or her age and intellectual and physical capacity should assume and is carrying them out. Mental health includes emotional stability and maturity of character as well as the strength to withstand the stresses of living without undue or persistent symptoms, physical or psychological. Mental health implies the ability to judge reality accurately and to see things in terms of long-term rather than short-term values. It implies the ability to love, to be able to sustain affectionate relationships with other persons. It means the ability to work in one's chosen field both pleasurably and productively. It demands the presence of an effective conscience, realistic and independent, and at the same time a practical code by which to live. Finally, it entails the gratification of certain basic needs — such as hunger, thirst, self-assertiveness and sex — in such a way as to not hurt other people or one's self."

Harvard's Dr. Dana Farnsworth has said that mental health is not freedom from anxiety, tension, dissatisfaction, or from all man's other negative states. Nor is it conformity, lack of stress, or constant happiness. "Perhaps it can best be defined as the state which permits an individual the freedom to interact positively with his environment and be capable of loving and working and playing," he believes. "It is the ability to carry on self-determined activities with satisfaction to one's self and with a sense of responsibility to others. All persons, mentally healthy or mentally ill, are obliged to suffer in various ways. By his nature, man cannot help but experience frustration, grief, pain, conflict, jealousy and fear.

These emotions, as well as others, can be important stimuli to effective and constructive action. Happiness is often a by-product of resolving, in part or in whole, exasperating and difficult situations."

Dr. Farnsworth feels that the level of mental health in a community is reflected in all its organizations and facilities. There are, he says, a number of symptoms of a low level of mental health, including a large incidence of conflict of various kinds, low morale, impersonality in human relationships, racism, poverty, drug abuse, a high rate of impersonal sexuality and confusion of sex roles, and excessive absenteeism in industry and schools. Indications of a high level of mental health, on the other hand, include adequate income, a general attitude of enjoyment and satisfaction, full use of resources without exploitation, self-control, cooperation, and equal opportunity. "Mental health," says Dr. Farnsworth, "as much or more than physical health, is involved not just with the individual but with his environment and with the foundation laid in the earliest months of his life."

He suggests that there are two tasks for any group, person, or society that wishes to engage in the primary prevention of crippling mental illness: to identify and work toward removing those environmental situations that cause such great stress that people cannot live with them constructively; to work toward establishing those conditions that strengthen personality development in infancy, encourage strong character formation in youth, and that support the "idealistic and altruistic attitudes so necessary in any society if it is to sustain itself successfully."

Selected
Bibliography

Asimov, Isaac. *The Human Brain: Its Capacities and Functions.* Boston: Houghton Mifflin, 1964.

Brussel, James A. *The Layman's Guide to Psychiatry.* New York: Barnes & Noble, 1961.

Callwood, Jane. *Love, Hate, Fear, Anger and the Other Lively Emotions.* New York: Doubleday, 1964.

Grossman, Frances K. *Brothers and Sisters of Retarded Children: An Exploratory Study.* Syracuse: Syracuse University Press, 1972.

Lerner, Barbara. *Therapy in the Ghetto.* Baltimore: Johns Hopkins Press, 1972.

Lewis, Howard R., and Lewis, Martha E. *Psychosomatics: How Your Emotions Can Damage Your Health.* New York: Viking Press, 1972.

McQuade, Walter. "What Stress Can Do to You." *Fortune,* January 1972.

Miller, Benjamin F., and Galton, Lawrence. *The Family Book of Preventive Medicine.* New York: Simon & Schuster, 1971.

The Mind. Life Science Library. New York: Time, Inc., 1972.

A Psychiatric Glossary. American Psychiatric Association, Committee on Public Information.

Scarf, Maggie. "Normality Is a Square Circle or a Four-Sided Triangle." *New York Times Magazine,* October 3, 1971.

Stevens, Peter H. *Emotional Crises.* New York: Odyssey Press, 1965.

Szasz, Thomas S. *The Manufacture of Madness.* New York: Harper & Row, 1970.

Today's Health Guide. American Medical Association, 1965.

Watson, George. *Nutrition and Your Mind.* New York: Harper & Row, 1972.

Index

Index

Index

lobotomy, 60, 144; *see also* psychosurgery

LSD (lysergic acid diethylamide), 55, 56, 82

lunacy. *See* mental illness

lyssophobia, 23

McBride, William, 81

McGarry, Louis A., 158

McKinney, William T., 24

McNaghten Rule, 7

malnutrition, 73, 84, 85, 86–88, 89–90; kwashiorkor, 86–87; marasmus, 87; and poverty, 89–90, 92

manic-depression, 11–12, 39, 40, 141, 142, 150–151, 156

Manufacture of Madness, The, 154, 155

Mark, Vernon, 110, 114, 115

masochism, 40

Massachusetts General Hospital, 81, 106, 107, 110, 116

Medical Aspects of Human Sexuality, 36

Medical Committee for Human Rights, 114

Medical Tribune, 23, 143

Medical World News, 36, 80, 144

Mehrle, Paul, 74, 75

Meierhofer, Marie, 23–24

Menninger, W. Walter, 10

Menninger Clinic, 10

Menninger Foundation, 128, 130

mental health, 116; definitions of, 159, 160–161

mental illness: causes, 3, 10–11, 12, 13, 35–36, 37, 39, 46–47, 50, 51, 52–53, 54, 56–59, 73–78, 82–85, 86–88; in childhood, 23–24, 64; definitions, 8, 14–15, 67; environmental factors, 47, 52, 73; functional, 10–11; hereditary factors, 50, 51, 52, 75, 84; his-

tory, 4–7; incidence of, 3, 8–10, 23, 34, 43–44, 48, 50–51, 63–64, 68, 74, 79, 83–84, 92, 117, 126; kinds, 11; legislation, 7–8; as myth, 154–156; organic, 10–11, 12, 13, 56–59, 73–78, 82–85, 86–88; and radiation, 13; reform, 5–7; research, 24–25, 50–51, 52–53, 54–59, 63–64, 74–75, 100, 105–106, 110–112, 118–119; treatment, 59–66, 120–151; *see also* brain dysfunction; character disorder; mental retardation; neurosis; psychosis; psychosomatic disorder; schizophrenia

mental retardation, 54, 61, 67–92, 112, 120, 148, 149; causes, 73–78, 82–85, 86–88, 117; definitions, 67, 68, 73; mild, 69–70; moderate, 69–70; prevention, 90; profound, 69–70; severe, 69–70; sociocultural, 90

metabolism, defined, 77

metal imbalance, 58–59

metal poisoning, 73, 83, 108

methadone, 62

MGH News, 106

migraine headache, 94, 99, 103

Modigliani, Amedeo, 14

Money, John, 36

Mongolism, 76, 78, 79, 90, 113; *see also* Down's syndrome

Moreno, J. L., 147

moron. *See* mental retardation, mild

music therapy, 145, 147–148

mysophobia, 23

narcissism, 12

National Association for Mental Health, 9, 116, 152, 153

National Institute of Mental Health, 10, 51, 63, 126

necrophobia, 23

Index